1951

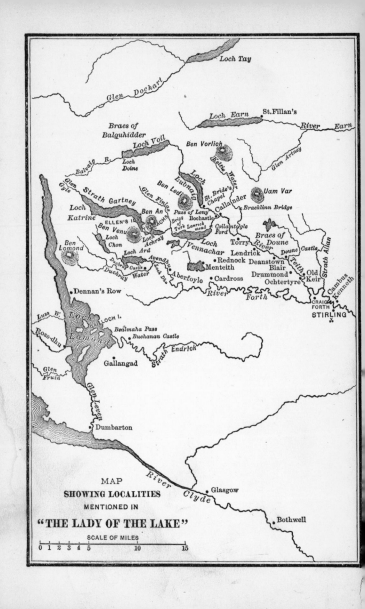

MAP

SHOWING LOCALITIES

MENTIONED IN

"THE LADY OF THE LAKE"

SCALE OF MILES

0 1 2 3 4 5   10   15

SCOTT'S

LADY OF THE LAKE

EDITED BY

HELEN E. BACON

DEPARTMENT OF ENGLISH, WADLEIGH HIGH SCHOOL
NEW YORK CITY

NEW YORK ·:· CINCINNATI ·:· CHICAGO
AMERICAN BOOK COMPANY

INTRODUCTION.

WALTER SCOTT, the ninth of a family of twelve children, was born at Edinburgh in August, 1771. His first consciousness of existence dated from the time when he was sent, a lame, delicate child, to Sandyknowe, the residence of his paternal grandfather. Here he "was often carried out and laid down beside the old shepherd among the crags or rocks round which he fed his sheep." If Scott's genius was late in flowering, who can say that the budding did not begin in that early, close companionship with the Highland country which he was to reproduce so vividly in his verse and fiction?

With strength increased by open-air life, although still slightly lame, we find him later a sturdy, active, not over-studious boy at school at Edinburgh and Kelso, and at fifteen beginning in his father's office the legal studies which he continued at the university.

Referring to the time after leaving the high school, when he made the acquaintance of Tasso's " Jerusalem Delivered," Percy's " Reliques," and the best works of English fiction, Scott says, " To this period I can trace distinctly the awakening of that delightful feeling for the beauties of natural objects which has never deserted me. From this time the love of natural beauty, more especially when combined with ancient ruins or remains of our fathers' piety or splendor, became within me an insatiable passion, which, if circumstances had permitted, I would willingly have gratified by traveling half over the globe."

His gigantic memory had always appropriated most eagerly the heroic and romantic elements of verse, tale, and history, from the days when, a child, he read Pope's translation of Homer aloud to his mother, to the time when he hunted ballads and chased traditions with the keen zest of a scholar and an antiquary.

The first notable outcome of these researches was his "Minstrelsy of the Scottish Border," published in 1802. To this collection of ancient Border ballads, which he had spent years in collecting, were added some spirited new ones which he had deftly shaped to the old models. This form of poetic expression was especially suited to the genius of Scott, and the class of subjects to which it was usually adapted had long been the object of his enthusiastic study.

The amplification, then, of the ballad to the proportions of the more pretentious metrical romance came by a natural process of crystallization of the elements of a rare power, profound research, and inspiring themes.

The first of the more ambitious efforts of Scott was the "Lay of the Last Minstrel," which was published in 1805. This became immediately and generally popular, and paved the way for the favorable reception of later productions. In 1808 "Marmion," the greatest poetical work of Scott, appeared. This was so enthusiastically received, that a certain friend urged him to be satisfied with such unexampled success, and refrain from publishing anything more, lest he impair his prestige. To this he replied, "If I fail, it is a sign that I ought never to have succeeded, and I will write prose for life: you shall see no change in my temper, nor will I eat a single meal the worse. But if I succeed,

> "'Up with the bonnie blue bonnet,
> The dirk, and the feather, and a'!'"

In this confident, buoyant spirit he made another venture, "The Lady of the Lake," published in 1810; and its extraordinary success justified his expectations. How sincere and widespread was the enthusiastic appreciation of this poem may be judged from the following instance, mentioned in Lockhart's "Life of Scott:" "In the course of the day, when 'The Lady of the Lake' first reached Sir Adam Fergusson, he was posted with his company on a point of ground exposed to the enemy's artillery, somewhere, no doubt, on the lines of Torres Vedras. The men were ordered to lie prostrate on the ground. While they kept that attitude, the captain, kneeling at the head, read aloud the description of the battle in Canto VI., and the listening soldiers only interrupted him by a joyous huzza when the French shot struck the bank close above them." We are not surprised at the soldierly tribute to the power of a poet "through whose head a regiment of horse had been exercising since he was five years old," whose sympathies had always been in touch with heroic achievement and chivalrous enterprise, and whose poems rang "with the quick, metrical tramp of his own moss-troopers;" but this was only a fractional though precious part of the applause that greeted him. "The whole country rang with the praises of the poet; crowds set off to view the scenery of Loch Katrine, till then comparatively unknown; and, as the book came out just before the season for excursions, every house and inn in that neighborhood was crammed with a constant succession of visitors."

Scott, in speaking of this poem, says, " The ancient manners, the habits and customs, of the aboriginal race by whom the Highlands of Scotland were inhabited, had always appeared to me peculiarly adapted to poetry. The change in their manners, too, had taken place almost within my own time, or at least I had learned many particulars concerning the ancient state of the Highlands from the old men of the last generation. I had also read a great deal, seen much, and heard more, of the romantic country where I was in the habit of spending every autumn; and the scenery of Loch Katrine was connected with the recollection of many a dear friend and merry expedition of former days. This poem, the action of which lay among scenes so beautiful, and so deeply imprinted upon my recollections, was a labor of love; and it was no less so to recall the manners and incidents introduced. The frequent custom of James IV., and particularly of James V., of walking through the kingdom in disguise, afforded me the hint of an incident which never fails to be interesting if managed with the slightest address or dexterity."

The high-water mark of Scott's popularity as a poet was reached with " The Lady of the Lake." In 1813 he published " Rokeby," and in 1814 " The Lord of the Isles." In the latter year " Waverley" appeared anonymously; and with this prose romance began Scott's career as a novelist, which extended through fourteen years. In this period of time he wrote twenty-three novels, besides some other works of minor importance.

" The land of the lakes and the mountains, and of the brave men," as the old Scots called their country, included the two great divisions, the Highlands and the Borders, which were so much wilder and more barbarous than the others, that they might be said to be altogether without law. Although nominally subject to the King of Scotland, yet they were so untamable that the enforcement of justice was almost as difficult as the subjugation of a foreign people.

The Highlands, rocky and mountainous parts of the country, comprised a large share of the north of Scotland. It was into these pathless wilds that the Romans drove the ancient Britons, and it was from these retreats that the fugitives afterward sallied forth to harass their conquerors.

The language of the Highlands, the Gaelic, was totally different from that of the Lowlands, which resembled English. The dress of the mountaineers also differed from that of the Lowlanders. They wore a plaid or mantle of frieze, or of a striped stuff called tartan, one end of which, being wrapped around the waist, formed a short petticoat, which descended to the knee, while the rest they folded around them like a sort of cloak. Their feet were covered with buskins made of rawhide; and the usual head covering was a cap called a "bonnet." They went always armed. Their weapons were bows and arrows, large swords, poleaxes, and daggers for close fight. For defense they had a round wooden shield, or target, stuck full of nails, and their great men had shirts of mail composed of links of iron. The common men sometimes wore a jacket of leather, having plates of metal stitched into it, but usually had no armor.

The Highlanders were divided into clans or tribes. All members of a clan supposed themselves to be descended from the same common ancestor, whose name distinguished them from other clans. Thus, one tribe was called MacDonald, which signifies the sons of Donald; another MacGregor, the sons of Gregor; MacNeil, the sons of Neil; and so on. They yielded unquestioning obedience to their chief, even when their submission to his orders implied disloyalty to the King. Each tribe had its own special territory, any invasion of which was punished as severely as though the foe had been of another nationality. Macaulay says of the sentiment that actuated them, "Their intense attachment to their own tribe and to their own patriarch, though politically an evil, partook of the nature of virtue. The sentiment was misdirected and ill-regulated, but still it was heroic. There must be some elevation of soul in a man who loves the society of which he is a member, and the leader whom he follows, with a love stronger than the love of life. It was true that the Highlander had few scruples about shedding the blood of an enemy; but it was not less true that he had high notions of the duty of observing faith to allies, and hospitality to guests."

The Highlanders were continually at war with the Lowlanders. They did not regard their plundering raids upon the richer grounds of the Lowlands as robbery, but as rightful recovery of possessions which had been wrongfully wrested from their ancestors. The Lowlanders, equal in courage and superior in discipline, could not be easily overcome, and thus there was almost constant war or discord between them.

Some of the more powerful Highland chiefs set themselves up as independent sovereigns, and even made alliances with the English in their own name. Macaulay says that "national enmities have always been fiercest among Borderers; and the enmity between the Highland Borderer and the Lowland Borderer along the whole frontier was the growth of ages, and was kept fresh by constant injuries." The Borderers were also divided into clans, and their devotion to their chieftain was complete. From their proximity to England, and their frequent incursions into its territory, they added to the perplexities of Scottish rule, which were already great by reason of constant internal dissension.

The Highlanders fought always on foot: the Borderers were all horsemen. The Borderers spoke the same language as the Lowlanders, wore the same sort of dress, and carried the same arms. Being accustomed to fight against the English, they were also much better disciplined than the Highlanders; but, in point of obedience, they were not much different from the clans of the north.

Military officers, called "wardens," were appointed along the Borders to keep these unruly people in order; but, as these wardens were generally chiefs of clans, they did not do much to mend the evil. The good Lord James of Douglas was intrusted with a great part of the charge of the Borders by Robert the Bruce. He was faithful to his trust, but the clan thus acquired power which was afterward dangerous to the country.

The hostility between the Highlanders and the Lowlanders was only equaled by the hatred both felt toward their Saxon neighbors, and it was not till 1745 that Scotland was subjugated by England. The conquest was so complete that even the national dress was abolished. The old Gaelic institutions and manners were modified, and the power of the clan chieftain was broken. With the last struggle of the exiled Stuart party, which ended in defeat at Culloden, began a new era for Scotland. To the old reign of lawlessness and disorder succeeded measures that were wisely coercive, and which finally secured a unity of Scottish interests, and greatly augmented prosperity in the entire kingdom.

In August, 1502, James IV. of Scotland married Princess Margaret Tudor, sister of Henry VIII. of England. It was hoped that this alliance would be the means of ending the bitter hostility which had existed between Scotland and England since the time of Edward I. A temporary peace ensued, but it was not till a century later that a descendant of the Scottish James sat on the throne of England.

The only son of James IV. and Margaret who survived infancy was James V. (James Fitz-James of the poem). He was born in 1513, and crowned when less than ten years old, his father having been slain at the battle of Flodden Field, which had resulted so disastrously for Scotland.

By the will of James IV., Margaret was to be queen regent as long as she remained a widow. In 1514 she lost the regency and greatly impaired her influence by marrying Archibald Douglas, Earl of Angus. Bitter enmity already existed between the head of the Douglas clan and other Scottish nobles; and, when Angus had the added dignity of being the husband of the queen regent, the jealousy and rivalry were greatly increased.

After losing the regency, Margaret was obliged to surrender the control of her son to Parliament. The Duke of Albany, the younger son of James III., was appointed regent during the minority of the King. Albany, who had spent many years at the luxurious court of France, returned to his native country with no appreciation of its real needs, and little sympathy with the Scotch. He failed to administer the government in a satisfactory manner. Angus plotted to secure control of affairs, and to gain custody of the young King. He assumed all the authority of a regent, without possessing any claim to the title, and kept James under close guard while pretending to govern the realm in his name.

The King was very restive under this irksome and unlawful restraint, and sympathized strongly with efforts which were made for his release. In 1526 two armed attempts were made to liberate him. Both resulted in failure. What could not be accomplished by force was finally secured by a cleverly planned stratagem of the royal captive; and he escaped to Stirling Castle, where devoted adherents awaited him. Two months later, Parliament declared the estates of the Douglases forfeited to the Crown, and there was neither place nor grace left in Scotland for any bearing the obnoxious name.

James even extended his animosity to one Archibald Douglas of Kilspendie (the Douglas of the poem), to whom he had been greatly attached. A touching story is told of the return of the old man, who had grown weary of his exile in England, and longed for a sight of Scotland and the former friendly regard of the King, whom he had never personally offended. He was doomed to undeserved disappointment, however, as James was unrelenting in his resentment, and would not modify any of the harsh conditions of his oath against the hated Douglas clan.

Although one of the most formidable obstacles to the exercise of royal rule disappeared with the crushing of the power of the Douglases, James still met much opposition from the nobility.

There were many abuses connected with the irregular rule exercised during his minority, and portions of the kingdom were in a condition of great lawlessness, which made it necessary for him to resort to severe measures. A five-years' truce was concluded with England in 1528, which allowed him to devote himself to the internal interests of Scotland. The following year he began to reduce the rebellious Borders to submission. By force and by craft he brought them into his power, putting to death many of the great nobles, and greatly limiting the privileges of those he allowed to live, until some degree of order was established.

After he had subdued the Borders, he proceeded against the Highland chieftains with equal rigor. The insubordination which had prevailed in that part of Scotland yielded to the unsparing severity of James, and life and property became measurably secure.

The King was greatly aided in the execution of his plans by the clergy, whom he favored in many ways, especially by countenancing the repression of heresy, — a course quite contrary to that pursued by his uncle, Henry VIII.

Popular sentiment also supported this " King of the Commons," as he was called from his habit of mingling with the common people, and taking a practical interest in their welfare. He was accustomed to travel over the kingdom in disguise, that he might learn the true condition of his subjects, and investigate the administration of justice. This custom, added to his fondness for hunting, gave him an intimate acquaintance with his kingdom and his people.

Scott says of him, " He was handsome in his person, and resembled his father in the fondness for military exercises and the spirit of chivalrous honor which James IV. loved to display. He also inherited his father's love of justice, and his desire to establish and enforce wise and equal laws. . . . He was a well-educated and accomplished man, and, like his ancestor James I., was a poet and a musician. He had, however, his defects. He avoided his father's failing of profusion, having no hoarded treasures to employ on pomp and show, but he rather fell into the opposite fault, being of a temper too parsimonious ; and, though he loved state and display, he endeavored to gratify that taste as economically as possible, so that he has been censured as rather close and covetous. . . . It must be added, that, when provoked, he was unrelenting even to cruelty; for which he had some apology, considering the ferocity of the subjects over whom he reigned. But, on the whole, James V. was an amiable man and a good sovereign."

Henry VIII. endeavored to enlist the aid of James in an organized resistance to the authority of the Church. The Scottish King apparently favored, in a measure, his uncle's policy; but his alliance with France restored and increased his adherence to papal rule.

The failure of James to keep an appointment made for meeting King Henry at York offended the latter, who accused him of dealing treacherously, and declared war against Scotland. Many of the Scottish nobles were disaffected, and the army was disorganized. At Solway Moss, James was openly defied by his nobility. Scott says regarding this bitter humiliation, "He shut himself up in the palace of Falkland, and refused to listen to any consolation. A burning fever, the consequence of his grief and shame, seized on the unfortunate monarch. They brought him tidings that his wife had given birth to a daughter; but he only replied, 'Is it so?' reflecting on the alliance which had placed the Stuart family on the throne. 'Then God's will be done. It came with a lass, and it will go with a lass.' With these words, presaging the extinction of his house, he made a signal of adieu to his courtiers, spoke little more, but turned his face to the wall, and died [1542] of the most melancholy of all diseases, a broken heart."

The story of "The Lady of the Lake" is briefly as follows:—

CANTO FIRST. — A huntsman who has distanced his companions and lost his steed, which, urged beyond endurance, has fallen dead in the Trosachs, has finally wandered over rocky ways to the shore of Loch Katrine. Here he winds his horn, hoping the sounds may reach his comrades. In response, a skiff appears rowed by a maiden, who thinks the blast was from her father's horn. Although at first startled, she is reassured by the "wildered wanderer's" explanation, and proffers the hospitality of her father's dwelling. They row across the lake to the island home, where, in the absence of the chieftain, Ellen, and the mistress of the mansion, the graceful Dame Margaret, dispense true Highland hospitality. He styles himself Knight of Snowdoun, James Fitz-James, but fails to learn the names of his hosts. "The stranger's bed of heather" was spread for the tired huntsman; but his rest was disturbed by "broken dreams," in which the exiled Douglases played a prominent part.

CANTO SECOND. — The stranger takes his leave in the early morning. Allan, the old minstrel, tunes his harp to a parting song, and Ellen watches the knight "wind slowly round the hill." Then, chiding herself for a momentary interest in him, she bids Allan sing in praise of the Græmes, one of whom is her lover. The old man is brooding over the ominous fallen sword, and cannot respond. He foresees the demand of Roderick Dhu, and distrusts the parting guest. Their conversation is interrupted by the music of the pibroch and the boat-song, which precede the landing of her cousin Roderick Dhu and his rough followers. Lady Margaret and her maids come to meet him. Ellen, quite willing to avoid her cousin, eagerly responds to her father's bugle horn, and hastens to meet him in her skiff. Malcolm Græme accompanies him. Roderick is informed that the King is preparing to deal with the Highland freebooters as severely as he has already done with the Border chieftains, and that the retreat of the outlawed Douglas has been discovered. Douglas is ready to withdraw with his daughter, thus lessening the danger of Roderick. The latter demands his alliance and the hand of his daughter. Both are refused by Douglas. A contest arises between Roderick and Græme, which results in the departure of the latter for the mainland, which he reaches by swimming from the island.

CANTO THIRD. — On the following morning occurs the consecration, with weird ritual, of the Fiery Cross. Roderick sends it forth by his henchman Malise to summon his followers to a gathering in Lanrick mead. It is borne eastward, passing from band to band, stopping for neither bridal nor burial, till the entire clan is summoned to the appointed place. The same morning Douglas departs with his daughter and Allan-Bane to seek refuge in the Goblin-cave on the side of Benvenue. Roderick passes the cavern on his way to the rally in Lanrick mead, and listens, as he lingers, to the sound of Ellen's voice in a hymn to the Virgin.

CANTO FOURTH. — The Highland clans have responded to the summons of the Fiery Cross. The Lowlanders are at Doune, ready to advance. Brian, the hermit monk, has tried a strange augury to determine on which side success shall be. He prophesies that that party shall be victorious which first sheds blood. Meantime Douglas has left his cavern retreat on some mission not made known to Ellen and Allan-Bane. They are instructed, however, to meet him at Cambus-kenneth if he does not return by nightfall. Ellen is anxious for her father's safety, believing he has gone to secure the release of Malcolm Græme. She scarcely heeds the song of Allan-Bane, who endeavors to cheer her. While they are speaking, Fitz-James appears. He declares his love for Ellen, and urges her to escape with him to Stirling. She replies by a frank avowal of her love for Malcolm Græme. The knight's sympathy is enlisted, and he leaves with her a ring, given him by the King for saving his life. This, he says, if presented to the King, will secure his protection for her and hers. Ellen and Allan-Bane endeavor to warn Fitz-James against the guide who departs with him. Their suspicions are confirmed by Blanche of Devan, a woman who has been half crazed since Roderick Dhu murdered her bridegroom in a wild Lowland raid. Her incoherent song is meant as a warning to the wandering knight in the Lowland dress. He charges Murdoch with treacherous intent. The guide seeks to escape, but not without aiming an arrow at Fitz-James. It grazes his crest, and lodges in the heart of Blanche of Devan. Fitz-James slays Murdoch, and returns to soothe the dying maniac. He promises to avenge her, and fastens to his bonnet a braid of her own and her bridegroom's hair, which he has dipped in her blood. Continuing his way alone after nightfall, he comes upon the camp fire of a stranger, who gives him shelter till morning, when he promises to lead him on his journey.

CANTO FIFTH. — After a night's rest and a hasty "soldier meal" in the morning, the Gael conducts his guest on his way, in accordance with his promise and Highland custom. Fitz-James allays the mountaineer's apprehension of an attack by the King, but declares his hostility to Roderick Dhu, and avows his eagerness to meet him in combat. The guide is incensed at this, and sounds a signal which brings to sight armed men on every side. He then reveals himself as Roderick Dhu. He is bound by his word to conduct his guest to Coilantogle ford, and therefore dismisses his followers. When this place is reached, Roderick challenges Fitz-James, and a deadly combat ensues. Throwing away his shield, that his arms may not exceed those of his adversary, he trusts to his sword alone. Fitz-

James is superior to his enemy through his knowledge of fencing, and finally overpowers him.

Fitz-James winds his horn, which is answered by four mounted attendants. He leaves the wounded man with two of them, with orders to bring him to Stirling, and hastens towards the Castle with the others. As they approach it, they perceive Douglas, who comes to surrender himself to the King, hoping thereby to secure the release of Malcolm Græme and avert the danger that threatens Roderick Dhu. The town is preparing for the burghers' sports, in which Douglas decides to join in order that he may attract the attention of the King. He surpasses all other competitors, and receives the prize from the King, who does not recognize him. Douglas endures this in silence, but he cannot refrain from resenting a huntsman's cruelty to Lufra, the hound, Ellen's companion. This results in his being seized and taken as a prisoner to the Castle. Meantime a messenger brings to the King tidings of the rising of Clan-Alpine. He sends a hasty message to avert an encounter, as Roderick is already his prisoner in Stirling stronghold.

CANTO SIXTH. — "This canto introduces us to the guard room in Stirling Castle, amid the remains of the debauch which has followed the games of the previous day. While the few soldiers who remain awake are finishing their carouse, and talking over the rumors of yesterday's battle, they are joined by one of their mates, who has been in the field, and brings with him a maiden and a minstrel (Ellen and Allan-Bane). They are at first disposed to treat the maiden roughly; but the sight of her innocent beauty, and her story of misfortune, touch the heart of one of the roughest in the company, who becomes her champion. Presently they are joined by the officer of the guard, who, at first

sight of Fitz-James's ring, commits the lady to proper care, while
John of Brent, the guardsman who had interfered, grants Allan's
request to see his master; but, fancying that the minstrel is one
of Roderick's clansmen, he shows him into the wrong cell, where
he finds the wounded chief. After anxious inquiries as to the
safety of his kindred, Roderick asks anew of the fight; and the
minstrel, in spirited verse, sings of the battle of Beal' an Duine,
whose issue was left doubtful by the arrival of a messenger from
the King with orders to stay the fight. But before he had fin-
ished his song the stern spirit had fled, and the minstrel's harp
changes its tune from battle song to death dirge.

"Meanwhile Ellen waits anxiously and impatiently for her
audience with the King. At last Fitz-James appears to escort
her to the audience chamber. Faltering, she looks round to find
the King, and sees, to her surprise, that her companion alone
remains covered, and 'Snowdoun's Knight is Scotland's King.'
He tells her how the feud with Douglas is at an end, and that
her father is now to be 'the friend and bulwark of his throne.'
But she still has the ring, still some boon to ask. She begs for
Roderick's life, but that is past giving; and when she shrinks
from further request, the King calls forth Malcolm, and throws
over him a golden chain, which he gives to Ellen to keep."—
R. W. Taylor.

THE LADY OF THE LAKE.

CANTO FIRST.

THE CHASE.

HARP of the North![1] that moldering long hast hung
  On the witch-elm [2] that shades St. Fillan's [3] spring,
And down the fitful breeze thy numbers flung,
  Till envious ivy did around thee cling,
Muffling with verdant ringlet every string,—
  O minstrel Harp! still must thine accents sleep?
Mid rustling leaves and fountain's murmuring,
  Still must thy sweeter sounds their silence keep,
Nor bid a warrior smile, nor teach a maid to weep?

Not thus, in ancient days of Caledon,[4]
  Was thy voice mute amid the festal crowd,
When lay of hopeless love, or glory won,
  Aroused the fearful, or subdued the proud.

---

[1] The poet invokes the spirit that animated the ancient Scottish minstrels, whose songs were usually accompanied by the music of the harp.

[2] Called also the " wizard elm," because forked twigs from the tree were used as divining rods.

[3] A Scotch abbot of the seventh century.

[4] The Romans gave the name Caledonia to that part of Scotland north of the Clyde and Forth.

At each according pause, was heard aloud
    Thine ardent symphony sublime and high!
Fair dames and crested chiefs attention bow'd;
    For still the burden of thy minstrelsy
Was Knighthood's dauntless deed, and Beauty's matchless eye.

Oh, wake once more! how rude soe'er the hand
    That ventures o'er thy magic maze to stray;
Oh, wake once more! though scarce my skill command
    Some feeble echoing of thine earlier lay:
Though harsh and faint, and soon to die away,
    And all unworthy of thy nobler strain,
Yet if one heart throb higher at its sway,
    The wizard note has not been touch'd in vain.
Then silent be no more!   Enchantress, wake again!

I.

THE stag at eve had drunk his fill,
Where danced the moon on Monan's [1] rill,
And deep his midnight lair had made
In lone Glenartney's [2] hazel shade;
But, when the sun his beacon red
Had kindled on Benvoirlich's [2] head,
The deep-mouth'd bloodhound's heavy bay
Resounded up the rocky way,
And faint, from farther distance borne,
Were heard the clanging hoof and horn.

II.

As Chief, who hears his warder [3] call,
"To arms! the foemen storm the wall,"

---

[1] St. Monan was a Scotch monk of the fourth century. The rill cannot be
identified.   [2] See map, p. 2.

[3] For the meaning of technical terms, colloquialisms, and unusual words
not to be found in a school dictionary, see *Glossary* at the end of volume.

The antler'd monarch of the waste
Sprung from his heathery[1] couch in haste.
But, ere his fleet career he took,
The dewdrops from his flanks he shook;
Like crested leader proud and high,
Toss'd his beam'd[2] frontlet to the sky;
A moment gazed adown the dale,
A moment snuff'd the tainted gale,[3]
A moment listen'd to the cry,
That thicken'd as the chase drew nigh;
Then, as the headmost foes appear'd,
With one brave bound the copse he clear'd,
And, stretching forward free and far,
Sought the wild heaths of Uam-Var.[4]

III.

Yell'd on the view the opening[5] pack;
Rock, glen, and cavern, paid them back;
To many a mingled sound at once
The awaken'd mountain gave response.
A hundred dogs bay'd deep and strong,
Clatter'd a hundred steeds along,
Their peal the merry horns rung out,
A hundred voices join'd the shout;
With hark and whoop and wild halloo,
No rest Benvoirlich's echoes knew.
Far from the tumult fled the roe,
Close in her covert cower'd the doe,

---

[1] The heath or heather is a small evergreen shrub very common in the Scottish Highlands.

[2] The head of a stag is said to be beamed after its fourth-year horns appear.

[3] "Tainted gale," i.e., the wind scented with the odor of the pursuers.

[4] See map, p. 2.

[5] A pack of hounds is said to "open" when the dogs begin to bark, upon recovering the scent or catching sight of the game.

The falcon, from her cairn on high,
Cast on the rout [1] a wondering eye,
Till far beyond her piercing ken [2]
The hurricane had swept the glen.
Faint, and more faint, its failing din
Return'd from cavern, cliff, and linn, [3]
And silence settled, wide and still,
On the lone wood and mighty hill.

IV.

Less loud the sounds of silvan war
Disturb'd the heights of Uam-Var,
And roused the cavern, where, 'tis told,
A giant made his den of old;
For ere that steep ascent was won,
High in his pathway hung the sun,
And many a gallant, stay'd perforce,
Was fain to breathe his faltering horse,
And of the trackers of the deer,
Scarce half the lessening pack was near;
So shrewdly [4] on the mountain side
Had the bold burst their mettle tried.

V.

The noble stag was pausing now
Upon the mountain's southern brow,
Where broad extended, far beneath,
The varied realms of fair Menteith. [5]
With anxious eye he wander'd o'er
Mountain and meadow, moss and moor,

---

[1] A confused or boisterous gathering.   [2] Sight.
[3] A deep pool.   [4] Severely.
[5] Or Monteith, a picturesque district of Scotland watered by the river
Teith.

And ponder'd refuge from his toil,
By far Lochard or Aberfoyle.
But nearer was the copsewood gray,
That waved and wept on Loch Achray,
And mingled with the pine trees blue
On the bold cliffs of Benvenue.
Fresh vigor with the hope return'd,
With flying foot the heath he spurn'd,
Held westward with unwearied race,
And left behind the panting chase.

VI.

'Twere long to tell what steeds gave o'er,
As swept the hunt through Cambus-more; [1]
What reins were tighten'd in despair,
When rose Benledi's ridge in air;
Who flagg'd upon Bochastle's heath,
Who shunn'd to stem the flooded Teith, —
For twice that day, from shore to shore,
The gallant stag swam stoutly o'er.
Few were the stragglers, following far,
That reach'd the lake of Vennachar;
And when the Brigg [2] of Turk was won,
The headmost horseman rode alone.

VII.

Alone, but with unbated zeal,
That horseman plied the scourge and steel; [3]
For jaded now, and spent with toil,
Emboss'd with foam, and dark with soil,
While every gasp with sobs he drew,
The laboring stag strain'd full in view.

[1] An estate about two miles from Callander, on the wooded banks of the Keltie.   [2] Bridge.   [3] Spur.

Two dogs of black St. Hubert's breed,
Unmatch'd for courage, breath, and speed,
Fast on his flying traces came,
And all but won that desperate game;
For, scarce a spear's length from his haunch,
Vindictive toil'd the bloodhounds stanch;
Nor nearer might the dogs attain,
Nor farther might the quarry strain.
Thus up the margin of the lake,
Between the precipice and brake,[1]
O'er stock[2] and rock their race they take.

VIII.

The Hunter mark'd that mountain[3] high,
The lone lake's western boundary,
And deem'd the stag must turn to bay,[4]
Where that huge rampart barr'd the way;
Already glorying in the prize,
Measured his antlers with his eyes;
For the death wound and death halloo,
Muster'd his breath, his whinyard drew; —
But thundering as he came prepared,
With ready arm and weapon bared,
The wily quarry shunn'd the shock,
And turn'd him from the opposing rock;
Then, dashing down a darksome glen,
Soon lost to hound and Hunter's ken,
In the deep Trosachs'[5] wildest nook
His solitary refuge took.
There, while close couch'd, the thicket shed

---

1 Thicket; underbrush.   2 The trunk of a tree.   3 Ben Venue.

4 " Turn to bay," i.e., to face an antagonist when escape is no longer possible.

5 " The Trosachs " is the name now applied to the valley between Lochs Katrine and Achray.

Cold dews and wild flowers on his head,
He heard the baffled dogs in vain
Rave through the hollow pass amain,
Chiding the rocks that yell'd [1] again.

IX.

Close on the hounds the Hunter came,
To cheer them on the vanish'd game;
But, stumbling on [2] the rugged dell,
The gallant horse exhausted fell.
The impatient rider strove in vain
To rouse him with the spur and rein,
For the good steed, his labors o'er,
Stretch'd his stiff limbs, to rise no more;
Then, touch'd with pity and remorse,
He sorrow'd o'er the expiring horse.
"I little thought, when first thy rein
I slack'd upon the banks of Seine,[3]
That Highland eagle e'er should feed
On thy fleet limbs, my matchless steed!
Woe worth [4] the chase, woe worth the day,
That costs thy life, my gallant gray!"

X.

Then through the dell his horn resounds,
From vain pursuit to call the hounds.
Back limp'd, with slow and crippled pace,
The sulky leaders of the chase;
Close to their master's side they press'd,
With drooping tail and humbled crest;
But still the dingle's hollow throat
Prolong'd the swelling bugle note.

---

[1] Echoed back their barks or chidings.   [2] In.
[3] The river which flows through Paris, France.
[4] Be to (from the old verb *worthen*, "to become").

The owlets started from their dream,
The eagles answer'd with their scream,
Round and around the sounds were cast
Till echo seem'd an answering blast;
And on the Hunter hied his way,[1]
To join some comrades of the day;
Yet often paused, so strange the road,
And wondrous were the scenes it show'd.

XI.

The western waves of ebbing day
Roll'd o'er the glen their level way;[2]
Each purple peak, each flinty spire,
Was bathed in floods of living fire.
But not a setting beam could glow
Within the dark ravines below,
Where twined the path in shadow hid,
Round many a rocky pyramid,
Shooting abruptly from the dell
Its thunder-splinter'd pinnacle;
Round many an insulated[3] mass,
The native bulwarks of the pass,
Huge as the tower[4] which builders vain
Presumptuous piled on Shinar's plain.
The rocky summits, split and rent,
Form'd turret, dome, or battlement,
Or seem'd fantastically set
With cupola or minaret,
Wild crests as pagod[5] ever deck'd,
Or mosque of Eastern architect.

1 " Hied his way," i.e., hastened.
2 " The western waves," etc., i.e., the horizontal rays of the setting sun
3 Isolated.
4 The Tower of Babel (see Gen. xi. 1–9).
5 The many-storied tower-like temples of the Chinese and Hindoos are

Nor were these earth-born castles bare,
Nor lack'd they many a banner fair;
For, from their shiver'd brows display'd,
Far o'er the unfathomable glade,
All twinkling with the dewdrop sheen,[1]
The brier-rose fell in streamers green,
And creeping shrubs, of thousand dyes,
Waved in the west wind's summer sighs.

XII.

Boon[2] nature scatter'd, free and wild,
Each plant or flower, the mountain's child.
Here eglantine embalm'd the air,
Hawthorn and hazel mingled there;
The primrose pale and violet flower,
Found in each cleft a narrow bower;
Foxglove and nightshade, side by side,
Emblems of punishment and pride,
Group'd their dark hues with every stain
The weather-beaten crags retain.
With boughs that quaked at every breath,
Gray birch and aspen[3] wept beneath;
Aloft, the ash and warrior oak
Cast anchor in the rifted rock;
And, higher yet, the pine tree hung
His shatter'd trunk, and frequent flung,
Where seem'd the cliffs to meet on high,
His boughs athwart the narrow'd sky.
Highest of all, where white peaks glanced,
Where glist'ning streamers waved and danced,

---

called "pagodas." About each story there is a balcony decorated with pendants or numerous projecting points or crests.

[1] Bright.　　　[2] Kind; bountiful.

[3] The trembling poplar, so called from the trembling of its leaves, which move with the slightest impulse of the air.

The wanderer's eye could barely view
The summer heaven's delicious blue;
So wondrous wild, the whole might seem
The scenery of a fairy dream.

XIII.

Onward, amid the copse 'gan peep
A narrow inlet, still and deep,
Affording scarce such breadth of brim
As served the wild duck's brood to swim.
Lost for a space, through thickets veering,
But broader when again appearing,
Tall rocks and tufted knolls their face
Could on the dark-blue mirror trace;
And farther as the Hunter stray'd,
Still broader sweep its channel made.
The shaggy mounds no longer stood,
Emerging from the tangled wood,
But, wave-encircled, seem'd to float,
Like castle girdled with its moat;
Yet broader floods extending still
Divide them from their parent hill,
Till each, retiring, claims to be
An islet in an inland sea.

XIV.

And now, to issue from the glen,
No pathway meets the wanderer's ken,
Unless he climb, with footing nice,[1]
A far projecting precipice.
The broom's[2] tough roots his ladder made,
The hazel saplings lent their aid;
And thus an airy point he won,

---

[1] Careful.   [2] A bushy shrub common in western Europe.

Where, gleaming with the setting sun,
One burnish'd sheet of living gold,
Loch Katrine lay beneath him roll'd,
In all her length far winding lay,
With promontory, creek, and bay,
And islands that, empurpled bright,[1]
Floated amid the livelier light,
And mountains, that like giants stand,
To sentinel enchanted land.
High on the south, huge Benvenue
Down on the lake in masses threw
Crags, knolls, and mounds, confusedly hurl'd,
The fragments of an earlier world;
A wildering forest feather'd o'er
His ruin'd sides and summit hoar,
While on the north, through middle air,
Ben-an[2] heaved high his forehead bare.

XV.

From the steep promontory gazed
The stranger, raptured and amazed,
And, "What a scene were here," he cried,
"For princely pomp, or churchman's pride!
On this bold brow, a lordly tower;
In that soft vale, a lady's bower;
On yonder meadow, far away,
The turrets of a cloister gray;
How blithely might the bugle horn
Chide, on the lake, the lingering morn!
How sweet, at eve, the lover's lute
Chime, when the groves were still and mute!
And, when the midnight moon should lave
Her forehead in the silver wave,

---

[1] Used adverbially.   [2] "Little Mountain," east of Loch Katrine.

How solemn on the ear would come
The holy matins' [1] distant hum,
While the deep peal's commanding tone
Should wake, in yonder islet lone,
A sainted hermit from his cell,
To drop a bead [2] with every knell —
And bugle, lute, and bell, and all,
Should each bewilder'd stranger call
To friendly feast, and lighted hall.

XVI.

" Blithe were it then to wander here !
But now, — beshrew yon nimble deer, —
Like that same hermit's, thin and spare,
The copse must give my evening fare;
Some mossy bank my couch must be,
Some rustling oak my canopy.
Yet pass we that; the war and chase
Give little choice of resting place; —
A summer night, in greenwood spent,
Were but to-morrow's merriment:
But hosts may in these wilds abound,
Such as are better miss'd than found;
To meet with Highland plunderers here
Were worse than loss of steed or deer. —
I am alone; — my bugle strain
May call some straggler of the train;
Or, fall [3] the worst that may betide,
Ere now this falchion has been tried."

[1] The first canonical hour of the day in the Catholic Church, beginning properly at midnight. Here referring to the striking of the hour by the " cloister " bell.

[2] " Drop a bead," i.e., say a prayer. The rosary used by Catholics is a string of beads by which count may be kept of the prayers recited.

[3] Happen; befall.

XVII.

But scarce again his horn he wound,
When lo! forth starting at the sound,
From underneath an aged oak,
That slanted from the islet rock,
A damsel guider of its way,
A little skiff shot to the bay,
That round the promontory steep
Led its deep line in graceful sweep,
Eddying, in almost viewless wave,
The weeping willow twig to lave,
And kiss, with whispering sound and slow,
The beach of pebbles bright as snow.
The boat had touch'd this silver strand,
Just as the Hunter left his stand,
And stood conceal'd amid the brake,
To view this Lady of the Lake.
The maiden paused, as if again
She thought to catch the distant strain.
With head upraised, and look intent,
And eye and ear attentive bent,
And locks flung back, and lips apart,
Like monument of Grecian art,
In listening mood, she seem'd to stand,
The guardian Naiad [1] of the strand.

XVIII.

And ne'er did Grecian chisel trace
A Nymph, a Naiad, or a Grace, [2]
Of finer form, or lovelier face!

---

[1] (*Nā'yăd.*) In classic mythology, one of the lower female deities who presided over lakes, streams, and fountains, as the Nymphs presided over mountains, forests, and meadows.

[2] The Graces were in classic mythology three lovely sisters who attended Apollo and Venus.

What though the sun, with ardent frown,
Had slightly tinged her cheek with brown,—
The sportive toil, which, short and light,
Had dyed her glowing hue so bright,
Served too in hastier swell to show
Short glimpses of a breast of snow:
What though no rule of courtly grace
To measured mood had train'd her pace,—
A foot more light, a step more true,
Ne'er from the heath flower dash'd the dew;
E'en the slight harebell raised its head,
Elastic from her airy tread:
What though upon her speech there hung
The accents of the mountain tongue,—
Those silver sounds, so soft, so dear,
The list'ner held his breath to hear!

XIX.

A chieftain's daughter seem'd the maid;
Her satin snood,[1] her silken plaid,[2]
Her golden brooch such birth betray'd.
And seldom was a snood amid
Such wild luxuriant ringlets hid,
Whose glossy black to shame might bring
The plumage of the raven's wing;
And seldom o'er a breast so fair
Mantled a plaid with modest care,
And never brooch the folds combined
Above a heart more good and kind.

---

[1] A band used by Scottish maidens to bind the hair.

[2] (*Plāyed.*) Several yards' length of usually checkered woolen cloth called "tartan," which the Scottish Highlanders of both sexes wound about their bodies, and which formed a characteristic feature of their national costume.

Her kindness and her worth to spy,
You need but gaze on Ellen's eye;
Not Katrine, in her mirror blue,
Gives back the shaggy banks more true,
Than every freeborn glance confess'd
The guileless movements of her breast;
Whether joy danced in her dark eye,
Or woe or pity claim'd a sigh,
Or filial love was glowing there,
Or meek devotion pour'd a prayer,
Or tale of injury call'd forth
The indignant spirit of the North.
One only passion unreveal'd,
With maiden pride the maid conceal'd,
Yet not less purely felt the flame; —
Oh ! need I tell that passion's name ?

XX.

Impatient of the silent horn,
Now on the gale her voice was borne: —
" Father ! " she cried; the rocks around
Loved to prolong the gentle sound.
A while she paused, no answer came, —
" Malcolm, was thine the blast ? " the name
Less resolutely utter'd fell,
The echoes could not catch the swell.
" A stranger I," the Huntsman said,
Advancing from the hazel shade.
The maid, alarm'd, with hasty oar,
Push'd her light shallop [1] from the shore,
And when a space was gain'd between,
Closer she drew her bosom's screen;
(So forth the startled swan would swing,
So turn to prune [2] his ruffled wing.)

1 Boat.   2 Trim or arrange.

Then safe, though flutter'd and amazed,
She paused, and on the stranger gazed.
Not his the form, nor his the eye,
That youthful maidens wont to fly.

XXI.

On his bold visage middle age
Had slightly press'd its signet sage,[1]
Yet had not quench'd the open truth
And fiery vehemence of youth;
Forward and frolic glee was there,
The will to do, the soul to dare,
The sparkling glance, soon blown to fire,
Of hasty love, or headlong ire.
His limbs were cast in manly mold,
For hardy sports or contest bold;
And though in peaceful garb array'd,
And weaponless, except his blade,
His stately mien as well implied
A high-born heart, a martial pride,
As if a baron's crest he wore,
And sheathed in armor trode the shore.
Slighting the petty need[2] he show'd,
He told of his benighted road;
His ready speech flow'd fair and free,
In phrase of gentlest courtesy;
Yet seem'd that tone, and gesture bland,
Less used to sue than to command.

XXII.

A while the maid the stranger eyed,
And, reassured, at length replied,
That Highland halls were open still
To wilder'd[3] wanderers of the hill.

---

[1] Of wisdom.   [2] Need of food.   [3] Bewildered.

"Nor think you unexpected come
To yon lone isle, our desert home;
Before the heath had lost the dew,
This morn, a couch [1] was pull'd for you;
On yonder mountain's purple head
Have ptarmigan [2] and heath cock bled,
And our broad nets have swept the mere,[3]
To furnish forth your evening cheer."—
"Now, by the rood,[4] my lovely maid,
Your courtesy has err'd," he said;
"No right have I to claim, misplaced,
The welcome of expected guest.
A wanderer, here by fortune tost,
My way, my friends, my courser lost,
I ne'er before, believe me, fair,
Have ever drawn your mountain air,
Till on this lake's romantic strand
I found a fay in fairyland!"

XXIII.

"I well believe," the maid replied,
As her light skiff approach'd the side,—
"I well believe, that ne'er before
Your foot has trod Loch Katrine's shore;
But yet, as far as yesternight,
Old Allan-Bane foretold your plight,—
A gray-hair'd sire, whose eye intent
Was on the vision'd future [5] bent.
He saw your steed, a dappled gray,
Lie dead beneath the birchen way;

---

[1] Heather, of which the Highlanders' rude couches were made
[2] (*Tär'mĭ-gan.*)   The white grouse.   [3] Lake.
[4] Crucifix or cross of Christ.
[5] "Vision'd future," i.e., visions of the future.

Painted exact your form and mien,
Your hunting suit of Lincoln green,[1]
That tassel'd horn so gayly gilt,
That falchion's crooked blade and hilt,
That cap with heron plumage trim,
And yon two hounds so dark and grim.
He bade that all should ready be
To grace a guest of fair degree;[2]
But light I held his prophecy,
And deem'd it was my father's horn
Whose echoes o'er the lake were borne."

XXIV.

The stranger smiled:—"Since to your home
A destined errant[3] knight I come,
Announced by prophet sooth[4] and old,
Doom'd, doubtless, for achievement bold,
I'll lightly front each high emprise[5]
For one kind glance of those bright eyes.
Permit me, first, the task to guide
Your fairy frigate o'er the tide."
The maid, with smile suppress'd and sly,
The toil unwonted saw him try;
For seldom sure, if e'er before,
His noble hand had grasp'd an oar:
Yet with main strength his strokes he drew,
And o'er the lake the shallop flew;
With heads erect, and whimpering cry,
The hounds behind their passage ply.
Nor frequent does the bright oar break
The dark'ning mirror of the lake,

1 Lincoln green is a kind of cloth made in Lincoln.
2 " Fair degree," i.e., high rank.   3 Wandering.   4 True.
5 " High emprise," i.e., dangerous adventures.

Until the rocky isle they reach,
And moor their shallop on the beach.

XXV.

The stranger view'd the shore around;
'Twas all so close with copsewood bound,
Nor track nor pathway might declare
That human foot frequented there,
Until the mountain maiden show'd
A clambering unsuspected road
That winded through the tangled screen,
And open'd on a narrow green,
Where weeping birch and willow round
With their long fibers swept the ground.
Here, for retreat in dangerous hour,
Some chief had framed a rustic bower.

XXVI.

It was a lodge of ample size,
But strange of structure and device;
Of such materials, as around
The workman's hand had readiest found;
Lopp'd off their boughs, their hoar trunks bared,
And by the hatchet rudely squared.
To give the walls their destined height,
The sturdy oak and ash unite;
While moss and clay and leaves combined
To fence each crevice from the wind.
The lighter pine trees, overhead,
Their slender length for rafters spread,
And wither'd heath and rushes dry
Supplied a russet canopy.
Due westward, fronting to the green,
A rural portico was seen,

Aloft on native pillars borne,
Of mountain fir, with bark unshorn,
Where Ellen's hand had taught to twine
The ivy and Idæan vine,[1]
The clematis, the favor'd flower
Which boasts the name of virgin bower,
And every hardy plant could[2] bear
Loch Katrine's keen and searching air.
An instant in this porch she staid,
And gayly to the stranger said,
" On Heaven and on thy Lady call,
And enter the enchanted hall!"

XXVII.

"My hope, my heaven, my trust must be,
My gentle guide, in following thee."
He cross'd the threshold — and a clang
Of angry steel that instant rang.
To his bold brow his spirit rush'd,
But soon for vain alarm he blush'd,
When on the floor he saw display'd,
Cause of the din, a naked blade
Dropp'd from the sheath, that careless flung,
Upon a stag's huge antlers swung ;
For all around, the walls to grace,
Hung trophies of the fight or chase :
A target[3] there, a bugle here,
A battle-ax, a hunting spear,
And broadswords, bows, and arrows store,
With the tusk'd trophies of the boar.
Here grins the wolf as when he died,

---

[1] " Idæan vine," i.e., a translation of the Latin name of the red whortle-
berry, *Vitis Idæa;* but this is a shrub, and could not be " taught to twine."
[2] Which could.   [3] Small shield.

And there the wild cat's brindled hide
The frontlet of the elk adorns,
Or mantles o'er the bison's horns;
Pennons and flags defaced and stain'd,
That blackening streaks of blood retain'd,
And deerskins, dappled, dun, and white,
With otter's fur and seal's unite,
In rude and uncouth tapestry[1] all,
To garnish forth the silvan hall.

XXVIII.

The wondering stranger round him gazed,
And next the fallen weapon raised: —
Few were the arms whose sinewy strength
Sufficed to stretch it forth at length:
And as the brand he poised and sway'd,
"I never knew but one," he said,
"Whose stalwart arm might brook[2] to wield
A blade like this in battlefield."
She sighed, then smiled and took the word:
"You see the guardian champion's sword;
As light it trembles in his hand,
As in my grasp a hazel wand;
My sire's tall form might grace the part
Of Ferragus, or Ascabart;[3]
But in the absent giant's hold
Are women now, and menials old."

XXIX.

The mistress of the mansion came,
Mature of age, a graceful dame;

---

[1] Hangings used to decorate the walls of a room.   [2] Endure.
[3] Ferragus and Ascabart were two giants of romantic fable. The former appears in Ariosto's Orlando Furioso; the latter in the History of Bevis of Hampton. His effigy may be seen guarding the gate at Southampton.

Whose easy step and stately port
Had well become a princely court;
To whom, though more than kindred knew,[1]
Young Ellen gave a mother's due.
Meet welcome to her guest she made,
And every courteous rite was paid
That hospitality could claim,
Though all unask'd his birth and name.
Such then the reverence to a guest,
That fellest[2] foe might join the feast,
And from his deadliest foeman's door
Unquestion'd turn, the banquet o'er.
At length his rank the stranger names,
"The Knight of Snowdoun,[3] James Fitz-James; [4]
Lord of a barren heritage,[5]
Which his brave sires, from age to age,
By their good swords had held with toil;
His sire had fall'n in such turmoil,
And he, God wot,[6] was forced to stand
Oft for his right with blade in hand.
This morning with Lord Moray's[7] train
He chased a stalwart stag in vain,
Outstripp'd his comrades, miss'd the deer,
Lost his good steed, and wander'd here."

XXX.

Fain would the Knight in turn require
The name and state of Ellen's sire.
Well show'd the elder lady's mien

---

[1] Dame Margaret was Roderick Dhu's mother, but had acted as mother to Ellen, and held a higher place in her affections than the ties of blood would warrant.   [2] Bitterest.   [3] An old name of Stirling Castle.

[4] Fitz means " son " in Norman French.

[5] " By the misfortunes of the earlier Jameses and the internal feuds of the Scottish chiefs, the kingly power had become little more than a name."

[6] Knows.   [7] A half-brother of James V. (James Fitz-James).

That courts and cities she had seen;
Ellen, though more her looks display'd
The simple grace of silvan maid,
In speech and gesture, form and face,
Show'd she was come of gentle race.
'Twere strange in ruder rank to find
Such looks, such manners, and such mind.
Each hint the Knight of Snowdoun gave,
Dame Margaret heard with silence grave;
Or Ellen, innocently gay,
Turn'd all inquiry light away: —
"Weird women we! by dale and down [1]
We dwell, afar from tower and town.
We stem the flood, we ride the blast,
On wandering knights our spells we cast;
While viewless minstrels touch the string,
'Tis thus our charmed rhymes we sing."
She sung, and still a harp unseen
Fill'd up the symphony between.

XXXI.

SONG.

"Soldier, rest! thy warfare o'er,
    Sleep the sleep that knows not breaking:
Dream of battled fields no more,
    Days of danger, nights of waking.
In our isle's enchanted hall,
    Hands unseen thy couch are strewing,
Fairy strains of music fall,
    Every sense in slumber dewing.[2]
Soldier, rest! thy warfare o'er,
Dream of fighting fields no more:

---

[1] Hilly or undulating land.   [2] Refreshing.

Sleep the sleep that knows not breaking,
Morn of toil, nor night of waking.

" No rude sound shall reach thine ear,
    Armor's clang, or war steed champing,
Trump nor pibroch [1] summon here
    Mustering clan, or squadron tramping.
Yet the lark's shrill fife may come
    At the daybreak from the fallow,[2]
And the bittern [3] sound his drum,
    Booming from the sedgy shallow.
Ruder sounds shall none be near,
Guards nor warders challenge here,
Here's no war steed's neigh and champing,
Shouting clans, or squadrons stamping."

XXXII.

She paused — then, blushing, led the lay
To grace the stranger of the day.
Her mellow notes awhile prolong
The cadence of the flowing song,
Till to her lips in measured frame
The minstrel verse spontaneous came.

SONG CONTINUED.

" Huntsman, rest ! thy chase is done;
    While our slumbrous spells assail ye,
Dream not, with the rising sun,
    Bugles here shall sound reveille.[4]
Sleep ! the deer is in his den;
    Sleep ! thy hounds are by thee lying;

---

[1] The Highlanders' battle air, played upon the bagpipes.
[2] Untilled land.
[3] A kind of heron said to utter a loud and peculiar booming note.
[4] (*Rĕ-vāl′yĕ.*) The morning call to soldiers to arise.

Sleep ! nor dream in yonder glen,
　　How thy gallant steed lay dying.
Huntsman, rest ! thy chase is done,
Think not of the rising sun,
For at dawning to assail ye,
Here no bugles sound reveille."

XXXIII.

The hall was clear'd — the stranger's bed
Was there of mountain heather spread,
Where oft a hundred guests had lain,
And dream'd their forest sports again.
But vainly did the heath flower shed
Its moorland fragrance round his head;
Not Ellen's spell had lull'd to rest
The fever of his troubled breast.
In broken dreams the image rose
Of varied perils, pains, and woes:
His steed now flounders in the brake,
Now sinks his barge upon the lake;
Now leader of a broken host,
His standard falls, his honor's lost.
Then, — from my couch may heavenly might
Chase that worse phantom of the night ! —
Again return'd the scenes of youth,
Of confident undoubting truth;
Again his soul he interchanged
With friends whose hearts were long estranged.
They come, in dim procession led,
The cold, the faithless, and the dead;
As warm each hand, each brow as gay,
As if they parted yesterday.
And doubt distracts him at the view —
Oh, were his senses false or true ?

Dream'd he of death, or broken vow,
Or is it all a vision now ?

XXXIV.

At length, with Ellen in a grove
He seem'd to walk, and speak of love;
She listen'd with a blush and sigh,
His suit was warm, his hopes were high.
He sought her yielded hand to clasp,
And a cold gauntlet [1] met his grasp:
The phantom's sex was changed and gone,
Upon its head a helmet shone;
Slowly enlarged to giant size,
With darken'd cheek and threatening eyes,
The grisly visage, stern and hoar,
To Ellen still a likeness bore.—
He woke, and, panting with affright,
Recall'd the vision of the night.
The hearth's decaying brands were red,
And deep and dusky luster shed,
Half showing, half concealing, all
The uncouth trophies of the hall.
'Mid those the stranger fix'd his eye
Where that huge falchion hung on high,
And thoughts on thoughts, a countless throng,
Rush'd, chasing countless thoughts along,
Until, the giddy whirl to cure,
He rose, and sought the moonshine pure.

XXXV.

The wild rose, eglantine, and broom
Wasted around their rich perfume:
The birch trees wept in fragrant balm,

---

[1] A mailed glove used by warriors in the middle ages to protect their
hands from wounds.

The aspens slept beneath the calm;
The silver light, with quivering glance,
Play'd on the water's still expanse,—
Wild were the heart whose passion's sway
Could rage beneath the sober ray!
He felt its calm, that warrior guest,
While thus he communed with his breast:—
"Why is it at each turn I trace
Some memory of that exiled race?
Can I not mountain maiden spy,
But she must bear the Douglas eye?
Can I not view a Highland brand,
But it must match the Douglas hand?
Can I not frame a fever'd dream,
But still the Douglas is the theme?
I'll dream no more—by manly mind
Not even in sleep is will resign'd.
My midnight orisons said o'er,
I'll turn to rest, and dream no more."
His midnight orisons he told,[1]
A prayer with every bead of gold,
Consign'd to Heaven his cares and woes,
And sunk in undisturb'd repose;
Until the heath cock shrilly crew,
And morning dawn'd on Benvenue.

[1] Repeated.

CANTO SECOND.

THE ISLAND.

I.

AT morn the blackcock trims his jetty wing,
   'Tis morning prompts the linnet's [1] blithest lay,
All Nature's children feel the matin [2] spring
   Of life reviving, with reviving day;
And while yon little bark glides down the bay,
   Wafting the stranger on his way again,
Morn's genial influence roused a minstrel gray,
   And sweetly o'er the lake was heard thy strain,
Mix'd with the sounding harp, O white-hair'd Allan-Bane! [3]

II.

SONG.

"Not faster yonder rowers' might
   Flings from their oars the spray,
Not faster yonder rippling bright,
That tracks the shallop's course in light,
   Melts in the lake away,
Than men from memory erase
The benefits of former days;
Then, stranger, go! good speed the while,
Nor think again of the lonely isle.

---

[1] A small European song bird.

[2] (*Măt'in.*) Pertaining to the morning.

[3] Highland chieftains often retained in their service a bard or minstrel, who was well versed not only in the genealogy and achievements of the particular clan or family to which he was attached, but in the more general history of Scotland as well.

" High place to thee in royal court,
    High place in battled [1] line,
Good hawk and hound for silvan sport,
Where beauty sees the brave resort,
    The honor'd meed [2] be thine !
True be thy sword, thy friend sincere,
Thy lady constant, kind, and dear,
And lost in love's and friendship's smile
Be memory of the lonely isle.

III.

SONG CONTINUED.

" But if beneath yon southern sky
    A plaided stranger roam,
Whose drooping crest and stifled sigh,
And sunken cheek and heavy eye,
    Pine for his Highland home;
Then, warrior, then be thine to show
The care that soothes a wanderer's woe;
Remember then thy hap erewhile,
A stranger in the lonely isle.

" Or if on life's uncertain main
    Mishap shall mar thy sail;
If faithful, wise, and brave in vain,
Woe, want, and exile thou sustain
    Beneath the fickle gale;
Waste not a sigh on fortune changed,
On thankless courts, or friends estranged,
But come where kindred worth shall smile,
To greet thee in the lonely isle."

---

[1] Ranged in order of battle.   [2] Recompense.

IV.

As died the sounds upon the tide,
The shallop reach'd the mainland side,
And ere his onward way he took,
The stranger cast a lingering look,
Where easily his eye might reach
The Harper on the islet beach,
Reclined against a blighted tree,
As wasted, gray, and worn as he.
To minstrel meditation given,
His reverend brow was raised to heaven,
As from the rising sun to claim
A sparkle of inspiring flame.
His hand, reclined upon the wire,
Seem'd watching the awakening fire;
So still he sate, as those who wait
Till judgment speak the doom of fate:
So still, as if no breeze might dare
To lift one lock of hoary hair;
So still, as life itself were fled,
In the last sound his harp had sped.

V.

Upon a rock with lichens wild,
Beside him Ellen sate and smiled. —
Smiled she to see the stately drake
Lead forth his fleet [1] upon the lake,
While her vex'd spaniel, from the beach,
Bay'd at the prize beyond his reach?
Yet tell me, then, the maid who knows,
Why deepen'd on her cheek the rose? —
Forgive, forgive, Fidelity!
Perchance the maiden smiled to see

---

[1] Of ducks.

Yon parting lingerer wave adieu,
And stop and turn to wave anew;
And, lovely ladies, ere your ire
Condemn the heroine of my lyre,
Show me the fair would scorn to spy,
And prize such conquest of her eye!

VI.

While yet he loiter'd on the spot,
It seem'd as Ellen mark'd him not;
But when he turn'd him to the glade,
One courteous parting sign she made;
And after, oft the Knight would say,
That not, when prize of festal day
Was dealt him by the brightest fair
Who e'er wore jewel in her hair,
So highly did his bosom swell,
As at that simple mute farewell.
Now with a trusty mountain guide,
And his dark staghounds by his side,
He parts — the maid, unconscious still,
Watch'd him wind slowly round the hill;
But when his stately form was hid,
The guardian in her bosom chid —
"Thy Malcolm! vain and selfish maid!"
'Twas thus upbraiding conscience said, —
"Not so had Malcolm idly hung
On the smooth phrase of southern tongue;
Not so had Malcolm strain'd his eye,
Another step than thine to spy. —
Wake, Allan-Bane," aloud she cried,
To the old Minstrel by her side, —
"Arouse thee from thy moody dream!
I'll give thy harp heroic theme,
And warm thee with a noble name;

Pour forth the glory of the Græme!"[1]
Scarce from her lip the word had rush'd,
When deep the conscious maiden blush'd;
For of his clan, in hall and bower,
Young Malcolm Græme was held the flower.

VII.

The Minstrel waked his harp — three times
Arose the well-known martial chimes,
And thrice their high heroic pride
In melancholy murmurs died.
"Vainly thou bidst, O noble maid,"
Clasping his wither'd hands, he said,
"Vainly thou bidst me wake the strain,
Though all unwont to bid in vain.
Alas! than mine a mightier hand
Has tuned my harp, my strings has spann'd!
I touch the chords of joy, but low
And mournful answer notes of woe;
And the proud march, which victors tread,
Sinks in the wailing for the dead.
Oh, well for me, if mine alone
That dirge's deep prophetic tone!
If, as my tuneful fathers said,
This harp, which erst [2] St. Modan [3] sway'd,
Can thus its master's fate foretell,
Then welcome be the Minstrel's knell!

VIII.

"But ah! dear lady, thus it sigh'd
The eve thy sainted mother died;
And such the sounds which, while I strove

[1] The ancient and powerful family of Graham of Dumbarton and Stirling
supplied some of the most remarkable characters in Scottish annals.
[2] Long ago.   [3] A Scotch abbot of the seventh century.

To wake a lay of war or love,
Came marring all the festal mirth,
Appalling me who gave them birth,
And, disobedient to my call,
Wail'd loud through Bothwell's[1] banner'd hall,
Ere Douglases, to ruin driven,
Were exiled from their native heaven. —
Oh! if yet worse mishap and woe
My master's house must undergo,
Or aught but weal to Ellen fair
Brood in these accents of despair,
No future bard, sad Harp! shall fling
Triumph or rapture from thy string;
One short, one final strain shall flow,
Fraught with unutterable woe,
Then shiver'd shall thy fragments lie,
Thy master cast him down and die!"

IX.

Soothing she answer'd him — "Assuage,
Mine honor'd friend, the fears of age;
All melodies to thee are known,
That harp has rung or pipe[2] has blown,
In Lowland vale or Highland glen,
From Tweed to Spey.[3] — what marvel, then,
At times, unbidden notes should rise,
Confusedly bound in memory's ties,
Entangling, as they rush along,

[1] Bothwell Castle on the Clyde, nine miles from Glasgow, was the principal seat of the Earls of Angus, the elder branch of the Douglas family, until 1528, when James V. escaped from his virtual imprisonment by Angus acting as regent, and drove the Douglases into exile, confiscating their estates (see Introduction).   [2] Bagpipe.

[3] The river Tweed is on the southern boundary of Scotland. The Spey is a river of the extreme north.

The war march with the funeral song?—
Small ground is now for boding fear;
Obscure, but safe, we rest us here.
My sire, in native virtue great,
Resigning lordship, lands, and state,
Not then to fortune more resign'd,
Than yonder oak might give the wind;
The graceful foliage storms may reave,[1]
The noble stem they cannot grieve.
For me,"—she stoop'd, and, looking round,
Pluck'd a blue harebell from the ground,—
" For me, whose memory scarce conveys
An image of more splendid days,
This little flower, that loves the lea,
May well my simple emblem be;
It drinks heaven's dew as blithe as rose
That in the King's own garden grows;
And when I place it in my hair,
Allan, a bard is bound to swear
He ne'er saw coronet so fair."
Then playfully the chaplet wild
She wreath'd in her dark locks, and smiled.

x.

Her smile, her speech, with winning sway,
Wiled[2] the old Harper's mood away.
With such a look as hermits throw,
When angels stoop to soothe their woe,
He gazed, till fond regret and pride
Thrill'd to a tear, then thus replied:
" Loveliest and best! thou little know'st
The rank, the honors, thou hast lost!
Oh, might I live to see thee grace,
In Scotland's court, thy birthright place,

---

1 Snatch away.   2 Beguiled.

To see my favorite's step advance,
The lightest in the courtly dance,
The cause of every gallant's sigh,
And leading star of every eye,
And theme of every minstrel's art,
The Lady of the Bleeding Heart !" [1]

XI.

"Fair dreams are these," the maiden cried,
(Light was her accent, yet she sigh'd;)
"Yet is this mossy rock to me
Worth splendid chair and canopy;
Nor would my footsteps spring more gay
In courtly dance than blithe strathspey,[2]
Nor half so pleased mine ear incline
To royal minstrel's lay as thine.
And then for suitors proud and high,
To bend before my conquering eye,—
Thou, flattering bard ! thyself wilt say,
That grim Sir Roderick owns its sway.
The Saxon [3] scourge, Clan-Alpine's [4] pride,
The terror of Loch Lomond's side,
Would, at my suit, thou know'st, delay
A Lennox [5] foray — for a day."

[1] The Bleeding Heart was the cognizance of the Douglas family in memory of the heart of Bruce, which that monarch on his deathbed bequeathed to James Douglas, that he might carry it upon a crusade to the Holy City.

[2] A rustic Highland dance which takes its name from the strath or broad valley of the Spey.

[3] "The Scottish Highlander calls himself Gael, and terms the Lowlanders Sassenach or Saxons."

[4] Gregor, the progenitor of the clan MacGregor, was supposed to be the son of a Scotch King Alpine: hence the MacGregors are sometimes called MacAlpines.

[5] The district lying south of Loch Lomond.

XII.

The ancient bard his glee repress'd:
" Ill hast thou chosen theme for jest !
For who, through all this western wild,
Named Black [1] Sir Roderick e'er, and smiled ?
In Holy-Rood [2] a knight he slew ;
I saw, when back the dirk he drew,
Courtiers give place before the stride
Of the undaunted homicide ;
And since, though outlaw'd, [3] hath his hand
Full sternly kept his mountain land.
Who else dared give — ah ! woe the day
That I such hated truth should say —
The Douglas, like a stricken deer,
Disown'd by every noble peer,
Even the rude refuge we have here ?
Alas ! this wild marauding Chief
Alone might hazard our relief,
And, now thy maiden charms expand,
Looks for his guerdon [4] in thy hand ;
Full soon may dispensation [5] sought,
To back his suit, from Rome be brought.
Then, though an exile on the hill,
Thy father, as the Douglas, still
Be held in reverence and fear ;
And though to Roderick thou'rt so dear,
That thou mightst guide with silken thread,

[1] Dhu in Gaelic.

[2] " In Holy-Rood," i.e., in the very presence of royalty.   Holyrood was
the King's palace in Edinburgh.

[3] A person who had been outlawed, or declared without the protection of
the law, could not bring an action at law.   Any one could steal his property,
or even kill him, without fear of legal punishment.   [4] Reward.

[5] Roderick and Ellen, being cousins, could not marry without dispensation, or special license from the Pope.

Slave of thy will, this Chieftain dread,
Yet, O loved maid, thy mirth refrain!
Thy hand is on a lion's mane."

XIII.

" Minstrel," the maid replied, and high
Her father's soul glanced from her eye,
" My debts to Roderick's house I know:
All that a mother could bestow,
To Lady Margaret's care I owe,
Since first an orphan in the wild
She sorrow'd o'er her sister's child;
To her brave chieftain son, from ire
Of Scotland's King who shrouds [1] my sire,
A deeper, holier debt is owed;
And, could I pay it with my blood,
Allan! Sir Roderick should command
My blood, my life, — but not my hand.
Rather will Ellen Douglas dwell
A votaress in Maronnan's [2] cell;
Rather through realms beyond the sea,
Seeking the world's cold charity,
Where ne'er was spoke a Scottish word,
And ne'er the name of Douglas heard,
An outcast pilgrim will she rove,
Than wed the man she cannot love.

XIV.

" Thou shakest, good friend, thy tresses gray, —
That pleading look, what can it say
But what I own? — I grant him [3] brave,

[1] Shields.
[2] Kilmaronock, a village about two miles southeast of Loch Lomond, has
a chapel or convent dedicated to St. Maronnan, of whom little is remembered.
[3] " I grant him," i.e., I grant that he is.

But wild as Bracklinn's [1] thundering wave;
And generous — save [2] vindictive mood,
Or jealous transport, chafe his blood:
I grant him true to friendly band,
As his claymore is to his hand;
But oh! that very blade of steel
More mercy for a foe would feel:
I grant him liberal, to fling
Among his clan the wealth they bring,
When back by lake and glen they wind,
And in the Lowland leave behind,
Where once some pleasant hamlet stood,
A mass of ashes slaked [3] with blood.
The hand that for my father fought
I honor, as his daughter ought;
But can I clasp it reeking red,
From peasants slaughter'd in their shed?
No! wildly while his virtues gleam,
They make his passions darker seem,
And flash along his spirit high,
Like lightning o'er the midnight sky.
While yet a child, — and children know,
Instinctive taught, the friend and foe, —
I shudder'd at his brow of gloom,
His shadowy plaid, and sable plume;
A maiden grown, I ill could bear
His haughty mien and lordly air:
But, if thou join'st a suitor's claim,
In serious mood, to Roderick's name,
I thrill with anguish! or, if e'er
A Douglas knew the word, with fear.
To change such odious theme were best, —
What thinkst thou of our stranger guest?"

---

[1] A cascade on the Keltie.   [2] Unless.   [3] Quenched.

XV.

"What think I of him?   Woe the while
That brought such wanderer to our isle!
Thy father's battle brand, of yore
For Tine-man[1] forged by fairy lore,
What time he leagued, no longer foes,
His Border spears with Hotspur's bows,
Did, self-unscabbarded, foreshow
The footstep of a secret foe.
If courtly spy hath harbor'd here,
What may we for the Douglas fear?
What for this island, deem'd of old
Clan-Alpine's last and surest hold?
If neither spy nor foe, I pray
What yet may jealous Roderick say?
— Nay, wave not thy disdainful head,
Bethink thee of the discord dread
That kindled, when at Beltane[2] game
Thou ledst the dance with Malcolm Græme;
Still, though thy sire the peace renew'd,
Smolders in Roderick's breast the feud.
Beware!— But hark, what sounds are these?
My dull ears catch no faltering breeze;
No weeping birch, nor aspens wake,
Nor breath is dimpling in the lake;
Still is the canna's[3] hoary beard;
Yet, by my minstrel faith, I heard —
And hark again! some pipe of war
Sends the bold pibroch from afar."

---

[1] Archibald Douglas, so called because so many of his enterprises ended in *tine* (or "distress").   After being defeated by Harry Hotspur at Homildon Hill in 1402, he joined Hotspur in his rebellion against Henry IV., and in the following year was with him disastrously defeated at Shrewsbury.

[2] The Celtic festival celebrated about the 1st of May.

[3] A species of grass.

XVI.

Far up the lengthen'd lake were spied
Four darkening specks upon the tide,
That, slow enlarging on the view,
Four mann'd and masted barges grew,
And, bearing downwards from Glengyle,
Steer'd full upon the lonely isle;
The point of Brianchoil [1] they pass'd,
And, to the windward as they cast,
Against the sun they gave to shine
The bold Sir Roderick's banner'd Pine.[2]
Nearer and nearer as they bear,
Spears, pikes, and axes flash in air.
Now might you see the tartans brave,[3]
And plaids and plumage dance and wave:
Now see the bonnets [4] sink and rise,
As his tough oar the rower plies;
See, flashing at each sturdy stroke,
The wave ascending into smoke;
See the proud pipers on the bow,
And mark the gaudy streamers [5] flow
From their loud chanters down, and sweep
The furrow'd bosom of the deep,
As, rushing through the lake amain,
They plied the ancient Highland strain.

XVII.

Ever, as on they bore, more loud
And louder rung the pibroch proud.
At first the sound, by distance tame,
Mellow'd along the waters came,

---

[1] A promontory on the north bank of Loch Katrine.
[2] The badge or crest of the MacGregors.   [3] Gay.   [4] Scotch caps.
[5] Ribbons attached to the chanters or tubes of a bagpipe for decoration.

And, lingering long by cape and bay,
Wail'd every harsher note away;
Then, bursting bolder on the ear,
The clan's shrill Gathering they could hear;
Those thrilling sounds, that call the might
Of old Clan-Alpine to the fight.
Thick beat the rapid notes, as when
The mustering hundreds shake the glen,
And, hurrying at the signal dread,
The batter'd earth returns their tread.
Then prelude light, of livelier tone,
Express'd their merry marching on,
Ere peal of closing battle rose,
With mingled outcry, shrieks, and blows;
And mimic din of stroke and ward,
As broadsword upon target jarr'd;
And groaning pause, ere yet again,
Condensed, the battle yell'd amain;
The rapid charge, the rallying shout,
Retreat borne headlong into rout,
And bursts of triumph, to declare
Clan-Alpine's conquests — all were there.
Nor ended thus the strain; but slow,
Sunk in a moan prolong'd and low,
And changed the conquering clarion swell,
For wild lament o'er those that fell.

XVIII.

The war pipes ceased; but lake and hill
Were busy with their echoes still;
And, when they slept, a vocal strain
Bade their hoarse chorus wake again,
While loud a hundred clansmen raise
Their voices in their Chieftain's praise.
Each boatman, bending to his oar,

With measured sweep the burden[1] bore,
In such wild cadence as the breeze
Makes through December's leafless trees.
The chorus first could Allan know,
" Roderick Vich Alpine, ho ! iro !"
And near, and nearer as they row'd,
Distinct the martial ditty flow'd.

XIX.

BOAT SONG.

Hail to the Chief who in triumph advances !
  Honor'd and bless'd be the ever-green Pine !
Long may the tree, in his banner that glances,
  Flourish, the shelter and grace of our line !
      Heaven send it happy dew,
      Earth lend it sap anew,
    Gayly to bourgeon,[2] and broadly to grow,
      While every Highland glen
      Sends our shout back agen,[3]
  " Roderigh Vich Alpine dhu,[4] ho ! ieroe!"

Ours is no sapling, chance-sown by the fountain,
  Blooming at Beltane, in winter to fade ;
When the whirlwind has stripp'd every leaf on the
    mountain,
  The more shall Clan-Alpine exult in her shade.
      Moor'd in the rifted rock,
      Proof to the tempest's shock,
    Firmer he roots him the ruder it blow ;
      Menteith and Breadalbane,[5] then,
      Echo his praise agen,
  " Roderigh Vich Alpine dhu, ho ! ieroe !"

---

[1] Chorus.   [2] (*Bûr'jŭn.*) Sprout.   [3] Again.
[4] Black Roderick, a descendant of Alpine.
[5] The district north of Loch Lomond.

XX.

Proudly our pibroch has thrill'd in Glen Fruin,[1]
  And Bannochar's[1] groans to our slogan[2] replied;
Glen Luss[1] and Ross-dhu,[1] they are smoking in ruin,
  And the best of Loch Lomond lie dead on her side.
      Widow and Saxon maid
      Long shall lament our raid,
   Think of Clan-Alpine with fear and with woe;
      Lennox and Leven-glen
      Shake when they hear agen,
  "Roderigh Vich Alpine dhu, ho! ieroe!"

Row, vassals, row, for the pride of the Highlands!
  Stretch to your oars, for the ever-green Pine!
Oh that the rosebud that graces yon islands
  Were wreathed in a garland around him to twine!
      Oh that some seedling gem,
      Worthy such noble stem,
   Honor'd and bless'd in their shadow might grow!
      Loud should Clan-Alpine then
      Ring from her deepmost glen,
  "Roderigh Vich Alpine dhu, ho! ieroe!"

XXI.

With all her joyful female band,
Had Lady Margaret sought the strand.
Loose on the breeze their tresses flew,
And high their snowy arms they threw,
As echoing back with shrill acclaim,
And chorus wild, the Chieftain's name;
While prompt to please, with mother's art,
The darling passion of his heart,
The Dame call'd Ellen to the strand,

A valley and localities about Loch Lomond.   [2] Battle cry.

To greet her kinsman ere he land :
" Come, loiterer, come ! a Douglas thou,
And shun to wreathe a victor's brow ? "
Reluctantly and slow, the maid
The unwelcome summoning obey'd,
And, when a distant bugle rung,
In the mid-path aside she sprung : —
" List, Allan-Bane !   From mainland cast,
I hear my father's signal blast.
Be ours," she cried, " the skiff to guide,
And waft him from the mountain side."
Then, like a sunbeam, swift and bright,
She darted to her shallop light,
And, eagerly while Roderick scann'd,
For her dear form, his mother's band,
The islet far behind her lay,
And she had landed in the bay.

XXII.

Some feelings are to mortals given,
With less of earth in them than heaven :
And if there be a human tear
From passion's dross refined and clear,
A tear so limpid and so meek,
It would not stain an angel's cheek,
'Tis that which pious fathers shed
Upon a duteous daughter's head !
And as the Douglas to his breast
His darling Ellen closely press'd,
Such holy drops her tresses steep'd,
Though 'twas an hero's eye that weep'd.
Nor while on Ellen's faltering tongue
Her filial welcomes crowded hung,
Mark'd she, that fear (affection's proof)
Still held a graceful youth aloof ;

No ! not till Douglas named his name,
Although the youth was Malcolm Græme.

XXIII.

Allan, with wistful look the while,
Mark'd Roderick landing on the isle;
His master piteously he eyed,
Then gazed upon the Chieftain's pride,
Then dash'd, with hasty hand, away
From his dimm'd eye the gathering spray;
And Douglas, as his hand he laid
On Malcolm's shoulder, kindly said,
"Canst thou, young friend, no meaning spy
In my poor follower's glistening eye ?
I'll tell thee : — he recalls the day
When in my praise he led the lay
O'er the arch'd gate of Bothwell proud,
While many a minstrel answer'd loud,
When Percy's Norman pennon,[1] won
In bloody field, before me shone,
And twice ten knights, the least a name
As mighty as yon Chief may claim,
Gracing my pomp, behind me came.
Yet trust me, Malcolm, not so proud
Was I of all that marshal'd crowd,
Though the waned crescent [2] own'd my might,
And in my train troop'd lord and knight,
Though Blantyre [3] hymn'd her holiest lays,
And Bothwell's bards flung back my praise,
As when this old man's silent tear,
And this poor maid's affection dear,

---

[1] The battle flag which Earl Douglas won from Hotspur at Newcastle in
1388.   [2] A crescent was one of the badges of the Percies.
[3] An abbey near Bothwell Castle.

A welcome give more kind and true,
Than aught my better fortunes knew.
Forgive, my friend, a father's boast,
Oh ! it out-beggars [1] all I lost !"

XXIV.

Delightful praise ! — Like summer rose,
That brighter in the dewdrop glows,
The bashful maiden's cheek appear'd,
For Douglas spoke, and Malcolm heard.
The flush of shamefaced joy to hide,
The hounds, the hawk, her cares divide;
The loved caresses of the maid
The dogs with crouch and whimper paid;
And, at her whistle, on her hand
The falcon took his favorite stand,
Closed his dark wing, relax'd his eye,
Nor, though unhooded,[2] sought to fly.
And, trust, while in such guise she stood,
Like fabled goddess [3] of the wood,
That if a father's partial thought
O'erweigh'd her worth and beauty aught,
Well might the lover's judgment fail
To balance with a juster scale;
For with each secret glance he stole,
The fond enthusiast sent his soul.

XXV.

Of stature tall, and slender frame,
But firmly knit, was Malcolm Græme.

---

1 Causes to seem poor.

2 Hawks or falcons were trained to pursue small game during the middle ages. When not in flight, they were usually blinded by means of a hood adorned with little bells.

3 Ellen, surrounded by the hounds and with the falcon on her hand, is likened to Diana, the goddess of the chase, in Greek mythology.

The belted plaid and tartan hose
Did ne'er more graceful limbs disclose;
His flaxen hair, of sunny hue,
Curl'd closely round his bonnet blue.
Train'd to the chase, his eagle eye
The ptarmigan in snow could spy:
Each pass, by mountain, lake, and heath,
He knew, through Lennox and Menteith;
Vain was the bound of dark-brown doe
When Malcolm bent his sounding bow;
And scarce that doe, though wing'd with fear,
Outstripp'd in speed the mountaineer:
Right up Ben-Lomond could he press,
And not a sob his toil confess.
His form accorded with a mind
Lively and ardent, frank and kind;
A blither heart, till Ellen came,
Did never love nor sorrow tame;
It danced as lightsome in his breast,
As play'd the feather on his crest.
Yet friends, who nearest knew the youth,
His scorn of wrong, his zeal for truth,
And bards, who saw his features bold,
When kindled by the tales of old,
Said, were that youth to manhood grown,
Not long should Roderick Dhu's renown
Be foremost voiced by mountain fame,
But quail to that of Malcolm Græme.

XXVI.

Now back they wend their watery way,
And, "O my sire!" did Ellen say,
"Why urge thy chase so far astray?
And why so late return'd? And why"—
The rest was in her speaking eye,

"My child, the chase I follow far,
'Tis mimicry of noble war;
And with that gallant pastime reft
Were all of Douglas I have left.
I met young Malcolm as I stray'd
Far eastward, in Glenfinlas' shade.
Nor stray'd I safe; for, all around,
Hunters and horsemen scour'd the ground.
This youth, though still a royal ward,[1]
Risk'd life and land to be my guard,
And through the passes of the wood
Guided my steps, not unpursued;
And Roderick shall his welcome make,
Despite old spleen,[2] for Douglas' sake.
Then must he seek Strath-Endrick glen,
Nor peril aught for me agen."

XXVII.

Sir Roderick, who to meet them came,
Redden'd at sight of Malcolm Græme,
Yet not in action, word, or eye,
Fail'd aught in hospitality.
In talk and sport they whiled away
The morning of that summer day;
But at high noon a courier light
Held secret parley with the Knight,
Whose moody aspect soon declared
That evil were the news he heard.
Deep thought seem'd toiling in his head;
Yet was the evening banquet made,
Ere he assembled round the flame,
His mother, Douglas, and the Græme,

---

1 "Royal ward," *i.e.*, under the guardianship of the King, Douglas's
chief enemy.   2 Feud.

And Ellen too; then cast around
His eyes, then fix'd them on the ground,
As studying phrase that might avail
Best to convey unpleasant tale.
Long with his dagger's hilt he play'd,
Then raised his haughty brow, and said: —

XXVIII.

" Short be my speech; — nor time affords,
Nor my plain temper, glozing[1] words.
Kinsman and father, — if sueh name
Douglas vouchsafe to Roderick's claim;
Mine honor'd mother; — Ellen — why,
My cousin, turn away thine eye ? —
And Græme; in whom I hope to know
Full soon a noble friend or foe,
When age shall give thee thy command
And leading in thy native land, —
List all ! — The King's vindictive pride
Boasts to have tamed the Border-side,
Where chiefs, with hound and hawk who came
To share their monarch's silvan game,
Themselves in bloody toils were snared;
And when the banquet they prepared,
And wide their loyal portals flung,
O'er their own gateway struggling hung.[2]
Loud cries their blood from Meggat's[3] mead,
From Yarrow[3] braes,[4] and banks of Tweed,
Where the lone streams of Ettrick[3] glide,
And from the silver Teviot's[3] side;
The dales, where martial clans did ride,
Are now one sheep-walk,[5] waste and wide.

---

[1] Flattering.   [2] See Introduction, p. 13.
[3] A tributary of the river Tweed, on the Scottish Border.
[4] Hillsides.   [5] A sheep pasture.

This tyrant of the Scottish throne,
So faithless and so ruthless known,
Now hither comes; his end the same,
The same pretext of silvan game.
What grace for Highland Chiefs, judge ye
By fate of Border chivalry.
Yet more; amid Glenfinlas green,
Douglas, thy stately form was seen —
This by espial sure I know:
Your counsel, in the streight I show." [1]

XXIX.

Ellen and Margaret fearfully
Sought comfort in each other's eye,
Then turn'd their ghastly look, each one,
This to her sire, that to her son.
The hasty color went and came
In the bold cheek of Malcolm Græme;
But from his glance it well appear'd
'Twas but for Ellen that he fear'd;
While, sorrowful, but undismay'd,
The Douglas thus his counsel said : —
"Brave Roderick, though the tempest roar,
It may but thunder, and pass o'er;
Nor will I here remain an hour,
To draw the lightning on thy bower;
For well thou know'st, at this gray head
The royal bolt were fiercest sped.
For thee, who, at thy King's command,
Canst aid him with a gallant band,
Submission, homage, humbled pride,
Shall turn the monarch's wrath aside.
Poor remnants of the Bleeding Heart, [2]

---

[1] "Your counsel," etc., i.e., I would have your advice in the emergency
I indicate.   [2] See Note 1, p. 55.

Ellen and I will seek, apart,
The refuge of some forest cell,
There, like the hunted quarry, dwell,
Till on the mountain and the moor,
The stern pursuit be pass'd and o'er."

XXX.

"No, by mine honor," Roderick said,
"So help me Heaven, and my good blade!
No, never!   Blasted be yon Pine,
My fathers' ancient crest and mine,
If from its shade in danger part
The lineage of the Bleeding Heart!
Hear my blunt speech: grant me this maid
To wife, thy counsel to mine aid;
To Douglas, leagued with Roderick Dhu,
Will friends and allies flock enow;[1]
Like cause of doubt, distrust, and grief,
Will bind to us each Western Chief.
When the loud pipes my bridal tell,
The Links of Forth[2] shall hear the knell,
The guards shall start in Stirling's[3] porch;
And, when I light the nuptial torch,
A thousand villages in flames
Shall scare the slumbers of King James!
— Nay, Ellen, blench not thus away,
And, mother, cease these signs, I pray;
I meant not all my heat might say.
Small need of inroad, or of fight,
When the sage Douglas may unite
Each mountain clan in friendly band,

[1] Enough.

[2] The windings of the river Forth: hence the inhabitants of that region.

[3] Stirling Castle, on the Forth, below the junction of the Frith, was a favorite residence of the Scottish kings.

To guard the passes of their land,
Till the foil'd King, from pathless glen,
Shall bootless turn him home agen."

XXXI.

There are who have, at midnight hour,
In slumber scaled a dizzy tower,
And, on the verge that beetled o'er
The ocean tide's incessant roar,
Dream'd calmly out their dangerous dream,
Till waken'd by the morning beam;
When, dazzled by the eastern glow,
Such startler[1] cast his glance below,
And saw unmeasured depth around,
And heard unintermitted sound,
And thought the battled fence[2] so frail,
It waved like cobweb in the gale;—
Amid his senses' giddy wheel,
Did he not desperate impulse feel,
Headlong to plunge himself below,
And meet the worst his fears foreshow?—
Thus, Ellen, dizzy and astound,[3]
As sudden ruin yawn'd around,
By crossing[4] terrors wildly toss'd,
Still for the Douglas fearing most,
Could scarce the desperate thought withstand,
To buy his safety with her hand.

XXXII.

Such purpose dread could Malcolm spy
In Ellen's quivering lip and eye,
And eager rose to speak — but ere

1 The startled dreamer.
2 " Battled fence," i.e., battlemented rampart.
3 Astounded.   4 Conflicting.

His tongue could hurry forth his fear,
Had Douglas mark'd the hectic strife,
Where death seem'd combating with life;
For to her cheek, in feverish flood,
One instant rush'd the throbbing blood,
Then ebbing back, with sudden sway,
Left its domain as wan as clay.
"Roderick, enough! enough!" he cried,
"My daughter cannot be thy bride;
Not that the blush to wooer dear,
Nor paleness that of maiden fear.
It may not be — forgive her, Chief,
Nor hazard aught for our relief.
Against his sovereign, Douglas ne'er
Will level a rebellious spear.
'Twas I that taught his youthful hand
To rein a steed and wield a brand;
I see him yet, the princely boy!
Not Ellen more my pride and joy;
I love him still, despite my wrongs,
By hasty wrath, and slanderous tongues.
Oh, seek the grace you well may find,
Without a cause to mine combined."

XXXIII.

Twice through the hall the Chieftain strode;
The waving of his tartans broad,
And darken'd brow, where wounded pride
With ire and disappointment vied,
Seem'd, by the torch's gloomy light,
Like the ill Demon of the night,
Stooping his pinions' shadowy sway
Upon the nighted pilgrim's way:
But, unrequited Love! thy dart
Plunged deepest its envenom'd smart,

And Roderick, with thine anguish stung,
At length the hand of Douglas wrung,
While eyes that mock'd at tears before,
With bitter drops were running o'er.
The death pangs of long-cherish'd hope
Scarce in that ample breast had scope,
But, struggling with his spirit proud,
Convulsive heaved its checker'd shroud,[1]
While every sob — so mute were all —
Was heard distinctly through the hall.
The son's despair, the mother's look,
Ill might the gentle Ellen brook;
She rose, and to her side there came,
To aid her parting steps, the Græme.

XXXIV.

Then Roderick from the Douglas broke —
As flashes flame through sable smoke,
Kindling its wreaths, long, dark, and low,
To one broad blaze of ruddy glow,
So the deep anguish of despair
Burst, in fierce jealousy, to air.
With stalwart grasp his hand he laid
On Malcolm's breast and belted plaid:
" Back, beardless boy !" he sternly said,
" Back, minion ! hold'st thou thus at naught
The lesson I so lately taught ?
This roof, the Douglas, and that maid,
Thank thou for punishment delay'd."
Eager as greyhound on his game,
Fiercely with Roderick grappled Græme.
" Perish my name, if aught afford
Its Chieftain safety save his sword!"

1 " Checker'd shroud," i.e., his tartan plaid.

Thus as they strove, their desperate hand
Griped to the dagger or the brand,
And death had been — but Douglas rose,
And thrust between the struggling foes
His giant strength : — " Chieftains, forego !
I hold the first who strikes, my foe. —
Madmen, forbear your frantic jar !
What ! is the Douglas fall'n so far,
His daughter's hand is deem'd the spoil
Of such dishonorable broil ! "
Sullen and slowly they unclasp,
As struck with shame, their desperate grasp,
And each upon his rival glared,
With foot advanced, and blade half bared.

XXXV.

Ere yet the brands aloft were flung,
Margaret on Roderick's mantle hung,
And Malcolm heard his Ellen's scream,
As falter'd through terrific dream.
Then Roderick plunged in sheath his sword,
And veil'd his wrath in scornful word :
" Rest safe till morning ; pity 'twere
Such cheek should feel the midnight air !
Then mayst thou to James Stuart tell,
Roderick will keep the lake and fell,[1]
Nor lackey, with his freeborn clan,
The pageant pomp of earthly man.
More would he of Clan-Alpine know,
Thou canst our strength and passes show. —
Malise, what ho ! " — his henchman [2] came ;
" Give our safe-conduct [3] to the Græme."

---

[1] Rocky highland or mountain.
[2] An officer or secretary who attended closely on the chieftain (from *hengst*, or " horseman," i.e., groom).   [3] Passport.

Young Malcolm answer'd, calm and bold,
" Fear nothing for thy favorite hold ;
The spot an angel deigned to grace
Is bless'd, though robbers haunt the place.
Thy churlish courtesy for those
Reserve, who fear to be thy foes.
As safe to me the mountain way
At midnight as in blaze of day,
Though with his boldest at his back,
Even Roderick Dhu beset the track. —
Brave Douglas, — lovely Ellen, — nay,
Naught here of parting will I say.
Earth does not hold a lonesome glen
So secret, but we meet agen. —
Chieftain ! we too shall find an hour,"
He said, and left the silvan bower.

XXXVI.

Old Allan follow'd to the strand,
(Such was the Douglas's command,)
And anxious told, how, on the morn,
The stern Sir Roderick deep had sworn,
The Fiery Cross [1] should circle o'er
Dale, glen, and valley, down, and moor.
Much were the peril to the Græme,
From those who to the signal came ;
Far up the lake 'twere safest land,
Himself would row him to the strand.
He gave his counsel to the wind,
While Malcolm did, unheeding, bind,
Round dirk and pouch and broadsword roll'd,
His ample plaid in tighten'd fold,
And stripp'd his limbs to such array
As best might suit the watery way, —

1 See Note 4, p. 78.

XXXVII.

Then spoke abrupt: "Farewell to thee,
Pattern of old fidelity!"
The Minstrel's hand he kindly press'd,—
"Oh! could I point a place of rest!
My sovereign holds in ward my land,
My uncle leads my vassal band;
To tame his foes, his friends to aid,
Poor Malcolm has but heart and blade.
Yet, if there be one faithful Græme
Who loves the Chieftain of his name,
Not long shall honor'd Douglas dwell,
Like hunted stag, in mountain cell;
Nor, ere yon pride-swoll'n robber dare,—
I may not give the rest to air!
Tell Roderick Dhu, I owed him naught,
Not the poor service of a boat,
To waft me to yon mountain side."
Then plunged he in the flashing tide.
Bold o'er the flood his head he bore,
And stoutly steer'd him from the shore;
And Allan strain'd his anxious eye,
Far 'mid the lake his form to spy,
Darkening across each puny wave,
To which the moon her silver gave.
Fast as the cormorant could skim,
The swimmer plied each active limb;
Then landing in the moonlight dell,
Loud shouted, of his weal to tell.
The Minstrel heard the far halloo,
And joyful from the shore withdrew.

CANTO THIRD.

THE GATHERING.

I.

TIME rolls his ceaseless course.   The race of yore,
   Who danced our infancy upon their knee,
And told our marveling boyhood legends store,
   Of their strange ventures happ'd[1] by land or sea,
How are they blotted from the things that be !
   How few, all weak and wither'd of their force,
Wait on the verge of dark eternity,
   Like stranded wrecks, the tide returning hoarse,
To sweep them from our sight !   Time rolls his ceaseless course.

Yet live there still who[2] can remember well,
   How, when a mountain chief his bugle blew,
Both field and forest, dingle, cliff, and dell,
   And solitary heath, the signal knew ;
And fast the faithful clan around him drew,
   What time[3] the warning note was keenly wound,
What time aloft their kindred banner flew,
   While clamorous war pipes yell'd the gathering sound,
And while the Fiery Cross[4] glanced, like a meteor, round.

---

   1 " Ventures happ'd," i.e., adventures which happened.
   2 Those who.   3 " What time," i.e., when.
   4 When a chieftain wished to assemble his clan suddenly, he sent out a
swift and trusty messenger, bearing a symbol, called the Fiery Cross, con-
sisting of a rough wooden cross the charred ends of which had been quenched
in the blood of a goat.   All members of the clan who saw this symbol, and
who were capable of bearing arms, were obliged to appear in arms forthwith
at the appointed rendezvous.   Arrived at the next hamlet, the messenger
delivered the symbol and the name of the rendezvous to the principal person-

II.

The summer dawn's reflected hue
To purple changed Loch Katrine blue;
Mildly and soft the western breeze
Just kiss'd the lake, just stirr'd the trees;
And the pleased lake, like maiden coy,
Trembled but dimpled not for joy;
The mountain shadows on her breast
Were neither broken nor at rest;
In bright uncertainty they lie,
Like future joys to Fancy's eye.
The water lily to the light
Her chalice rear'd of silver bright;
The doe awoke, and to the lawn,
Begemm'd with dewdrops, led her fawn;
The gray mist left the mountain side,
The torrent show'd its glistening pride;
Invisible in flecked sky,
The lark sent down her revelry;
The blackbird and the speckled thrush
Good-morrow gave from brake and bush;
In answer coo'd the cushat dove
Her notes of peace, and rest, and love.

III.

No thought of peace, no thought of rest,
Assuaged the storm in Roderick's breast.
With sheathed broadsword in his hand,
Abrupt he paced the islet strand,
And eyed the rising sun, and laid
His hand on his impatient blade.

age, who immediately forwarded them by a fresh messenger. In this way
the signal for gathering was disseminated throughout the territory of a large
clan in a surprisingly short space of time.

Beneath a rock, his vassals' care
Was prompt the ritual[1] to prepare,
With deep and deathful meaning fraught;
For such Antiquity had taught
Was preface meet, ere yet abroad
The Cross of Fire should take its road.
The shrinking band stood oft aghast
At the impatient glance he cast;—
Such glance the mountain eagle threw,
As, from the cliffs of Benvenue,
She spread her dark sails on the wind,
And, high in middle heaven reclined,
With her broad shadow on the lake,
Silenced the warblers of the brake.

IV.

A heap of wither'd boughs was piled,
Of juniper and rowan[2] wild,
Mingled with shivers from the oak,
Rent by the lightning's recent stroke.
Brian, the Hermit, by it stood,
Barefooted, in his frock and hood.[3]
His grisled beard and matted hair
Obscured a visage of despair;
His naked arms and legs, seamed o'er,
The scars of frantic penance bore.
That monk, of savage form and face,
The impending danger of his race
Had drawn[4] from deepest solitude,
Far in Benharrow's[5] bosom rude.

---

[1] The ritual or religious ceremony with which the Fiery Cross was made.
[2] Mountain ash.
[3] " Frock and hood," i.e., the usual garments of monks or hermits.
[4] " That monk," etc., i.e., the impending danger . . . had drawn that monk, etc.   [5] A mountain near the head of Loch Lomond.

Not his the mien of Christian priest,
But Druid's,[1] from the grave released,
Whose hardened heart and eye might brook
On human sacrifice to look ;
And much, 'twas said, of heathen lore,
Mixed in the charms he muttered o'er.
The hallow'd creed gave only worse
And deadlier emphasis of curse ;
No peasant sought that Hermit's prayer,
His cave the pilgrim shunn'd with care,
The eager huntsman knew his bound,
And in mid-chase called off his hound ;
Or if, in lonely glen or strath,
The desert dweller met his path,
He pray'd, and signed the cross between,
While terror took devotion's mien.

v.

Of Brian's birth strange tales were told.
His mother watch'd a midnight fold,[2]
Built deep within a dreary glen,
Where scatter'd lay the bones of men,
In some forgotten battle slain,
And bleach'd by drifting wind and rain.
It might have tamed a warrior's heart,
To view such mockery of his art !
The knot-grass fetter'd there the hand,
Which once could burst an iron band ;
Beneath the broad and ample bone,
That buckler'd heart to fear unknown,
A feeble and a timorous guest,
The field-fare [3] framed her lowly nest ;

---

[1] The Druids were the priests among the ancient Celtic nations in Gaul and
Britain.   They worshiped in forests, regarded oaks and mistletoe as sacred,
and offered human sacrifices.   [2] Sheep pen.   [3] Bird.

There the slow blind-worm left his slime
On the fleet limbs that mock'd at time;
And there, too, lay the leader's skull,
Still wreathed with chaplet, flush'd and full,
For heath-bell, with her purple bloom,
Supplied the bonnet and the plume.
All night, in this sad glen, the maid
Sate, shrouded in her mantle's shade:
— She said, no shepherd sought her side,
No hunter's hand her snood untied,
Yet ne'er again, to braid her hair,
The virgin snood did Alice wear;
Gone was her maiden glee and sport,
Her maiden girdle all too short;
Nor sought she, from that fatal night,
Or holy church, or blessed rite,
But lock'd her secret in her breast,
And died in travail, unconfess'd.

VI.

Alone, among his young compeers,
Was Brian from his infant years;
A moody and heart-broken boy,
Estranged from sympathy and joy,
Bearing each taunt which careless tongue
On his mysterious lineage flung.
Whole nights he spent by moonlight pale,
To wood and stream his hap to wail,
Till, frantic, he as truth received
What of his birth the crowd believed,
And sought, in mist and meteor fire,
To meet and know his Phantom Sire !
In vain, to soothe his wayward fate,
The cloister oped her pitying gate;
In vain, the learning of the age

Unclasp'd the sable-lettered [1] page;
Even in its treasures he could find
Food for the fever of his mind.
Eager he read whatever tells
Of magic, cabala,[2] and spells,
And every dark pursuit allied
To curious and presumptuous pride;
Till, with fired brain and nerves o'erstrung,
And heart with mystic horrors wrung,
Desperate he sought Benharrow's den,
And hid him from the haunts of men.

VII.

The desert gave him visions wild,
Such as might suit the specter's child.
Where with black cliffs the torrents toil,
He watch'd the wheeling eddies boil,
Till, from their foam, his dazzled eyes
Beheld the River Demon [3] rise;
The mountain mist took form and limb,
Of noontide hag, or goblin grim;
The midnight wind came wild and dread,
Swell'd with the voices of the dead;
Far on the future battle heath
His eye beheld the ranks of death:
Thus the lone Seer, from mankind hurl'd,
Shaped forth a disembodied world.
One lingering sympathy of mind
Still bound him to the mortal kind;
The only parent he could claim
Of ancient Alpine's lineage came.

---

[1] Black letter, the name of the Old English or modern Gothic letters used in old manuscript and early printed books.   [2] Mysteries.

[3] A malicious spirit supposed by the superstitious Scotch people to inhabit lakes and rivers, and to forebode calamity.

Late had he heard, in prophet's dream,
The fatal Ben-Shie's[1] boding scream;
Sounds,[2] too, had come in midnight blast,
Of charging steeds, careering fast
Along Benharrow's shingly side,
Where mortal horseman ne'er might ride;
The thunderbolt had split the pine,—
All augur'd ill to Alpine's line.
He girt his loins, and came to show
The signals of impending woe,
And now stood prompt to bless or ban,[3]
As bade the Chieftain of his clan.

VIII.

'Twas all prepared;[4]—and from the rock,
A goat, the patriarch of the flock,
Before the kindling pile was laid,
And pierced by Roderick's ready blade.
Patient the sickening victim eyed
The lifeblood ebb in crimson tide,
Down his clogg'd beard and shaggy limb,
Till darkness glazed his eyeballs dim.
The grisly priest, with murmuring prayer,
A slender crosslet form'd with care,
A cubit's[5] length in measure due;
The shaft and limbs were rods of yew,
Whose parents in Inch-Cailliach[6] wave
Their shadows o'er Clan-Alpine's grave,
And, answering Lomond's breezes deep,

---

[1] A fairy supposed to indicate coming death or disaster by her lamenta-
tions.   [2] Sounds of the same foreboding character.   [3] Curse.

[4] The ritual referred to in Canto III. was all prepared.

[5] About eighteen inches.

[6] The Isles of Nuns in Loch Lomond, and place of burial of the descendants of MacGregor.

Soothe many a chieftain's endless sleep.
The Cross, thus form'd, he held on high,
With wasted hand, and haggard eye,
And strange and mingled feelings woke,
While his anathema he spoke.

IX.

"Woe to the clansman who shall view
This symbol of sepulchral yew,
Forgetful that its branches grew
Where weep the heavens their holiest dew
    On Alpine's dwelling low!
Deserter of his Chieftain's trust,
He ne'er shall mingle with their dust,
But, from his sires and kindred thrust,
Each clansman's execration just
    Shall doom him wrath and woe."
He paused; — the word the vassals took,
With forward step and fiery look,
On high their naked brands they shook,
Their clattering targets wildly strook;[1]
    And first in murmur low,
Then, like the billow in his course,
That far to seaward finds his source,
And flings to shore his muster'd force,
Burst, with loud roar, their answer hoarse,
    "Woe to the traitor, woe!"
Ben-an's gray scalp the accents knew,[2]
The joyous wolf from covert drew,
The exulting eagle scream'd afar, —
They knew the voice of Alpine's war.

---

[1] Struck.   [2] "Scalp," etc., i.e., summit the accents heard.

X.

The shout was hush'd on lake and fell,
The monk resumed his mutter'd spell:
Dismal and low its accents came,
The while he scathed [1] the Cross with flame;
And the few words that reach'd the air,
Although the holiest name was there,
Had more of blasphemy than prayer.
But when he shook above the crowd
Its kindled points, he spoke aloud: ——
"Woe to the wretch who fails to rear
At this dread sign the ready spear !
For, as the flames this symbol sear,
His home, the refuge of his fear,
    A kindred fate shall know;
Far o'er its roof the volumed flame
Clan-Alpine's vengeance shall proclaim,
While maids and matrons on his name
Shall call down wretchedness and shame,
    And infamy and woe."
Then rose the cry of females, shrill
As goshawk's whistle on the hill,
Denouncing [2] misery and ill,
Mingled with childhood's babbling trill
    Of curses stammer'd slow;
Answering, with imprecation dread,
"Sunk be his home in embers red !
And cursed be the meanest shed
That e'er shall hide the houseless head,
    We doom to want and woe!"
A sharp and shrieking echo gave,

---

[1] Scorched; charred.

[2] Upon the recreant who failed to respond to the "dread sign" of the Fiery Cross.

Coir-Uriskin,[1] thy Goblin-cave!
And the gray pass where birches wave
   On Beala-nam-bo.[2]

XI.

Then deeper paused the priest anew,
And hard his laboring breath he drew,
While, with set teeth and clinched hand,
And eyes that glow'd like fiery brand,
He meditated curse more dread,
And deadlier, on the clansman's head,
Who, summon'd to his Chieftain's aid,
The signal saw and disobeyed.
The crosslet's points of sparkling wood
He quenched among the bubbling blood,
And, as again the sign he rear'd,
Hollow and hoarse his voice was heard:
" When flits this Cross from man to man,
Vich-Alpine's summons to his clan,
Burst be the ear that fails to heed!
Palsied the foot that shuns to speed!
May ravens tear the careless eyes,
Wolves make the coward heart their prize!
As sinks that blood stream in the earth,
So may his heart's blood drench his hearth!
As dies in hissing gore the spark,
Quench thou his light, Destruction dark,
And be the grace to him denied,
Bought by this sign to all beside!"
He ceased; no echo gave agen
The murmur of the deep Amen.

---

[1] A ravine of Benvenue supposed to be haunted by evil spirits.
[2] The Pass of the Cattle, above Coir-Uriskin.

XII.

Then Roderick, with impatient look,
From Brian's hand the symbol took:
"Speed, Malise, speed!" he said, and gave
The crosslet to his henchman brave.
"The muster-place be Lanrick mead [1] —
Instant the time — speed, Malise, speed!"
Like heath bird, when the hawks pursue,
A barge across Loch Katrine flew;
High stood the henchman on the prow;
So rapidly the barge-men row,
The bubbles, where they launch'd the boat,
Were all unbroken and afloat,
Dancing in foam and ripple still,
When it had near'd the mainland hill:
And from the silver beach's side
Still was the prow three fathom wide,
When lightly bounded to the land
The messenger of blood and brand.

XIII.

Speed, Malise, speed! the dun deer's hide [2]
On fleeter foot was never tied.
Speed, Malise, speed! such cause of haste
Thine active sinews never braced.
Bend 'gainst the steepy hill thy breast,
Burst down like torrent from its crest;
With short and springing footstep pass
The trembling bog and false morass;
Across the brook like roebuck bound,
And thread the brake like questing [3] hound;

[1] A meadow at the western end of Loch Vennachar.
[2] The shoes or buskins of the Highlanders were made of this hide.
[3] Hunting.

The crag is high, the scaur is deep,
Yet shrink not from the desperate leap:
Parch'd are thy burning lips and brow,
Yet by the fountain pause not now;
Herald of battle, fate, and fear,
Stretch onward in thy fleet career!
The wounded hind thou track'st not now,
Pursuest not maid through greenwood bough,
Nor pliest thou now thy flying pace
With rivals in the mountain race;
But danger, death, and warrior deed
Are in thy course — speed, Malise, speed!

XIV.

Fast as the fatal symbol flies,
In arms the huts and hamlets rise;
From winding glen, from upland brown,
They pour'd each hardy tenant down.
Nor slack'd the messenger his pace;
He show'd the sign, he named the place,
And, pressing forward like the wind,
Left clamor and surprise behind.
The fisherman forsook the strand,
The swarthy smith took dirk and brand;
With changed cheer,[1] the mower blithe
Left in the half-cut swath the scythe;
The herds without a keeper stray'd,
The plow was in mid-furrow stayed,
The falc'ner toss'd his hawk away,
The hunter left the stag at bay;
Prompt at the signal of alarms,
Each son of Alpine rush'd to arms;
So swept the tumult and affray
Along the margin of Achray.

[1] State of mind.

Alas, thou lovely lake! that e'er
Thy banks should echo sounds of fear!
The rocks, the bosky[1] thickets, sleep
So stilly on thy bosom deep,
The lark's blithe carol, from the cloud,
Seems for the scene too gayly loud.

XV.

Speed, Malise, speed!   The lake is past,
Duncraggan's[2] huts appear at last,
And peep, like moss-grown rocks, half seen,
Half hidden in the copse so green;
There mayst thou rest, thy labor done,
Their lord shall speed the signal on. —
As stoops the hawk upon his prey,
The henchman shot him down the way.
— What woeful accents load the gale?
The funeral yell, the female wail!
A gallant hunter's sport is o'er,
A valiant warrior fights no more.
Who, in the battle or the chase,
At Roderick's side shall fill his place! —
Within the hall, where torch's ray
Supplies the excluded beams of day,
Lies Duncan on his lowly bier,
And o'er him streams his widow's tear.
His stripling son stands mournful by,
His youngest weeps, but knows not why;
The village maids and matrons round
The dismal coronach[3] resound.

---

[1] Bushy.
[2] An estate between Lochs Achray and Vennachar.
[3] The Scottish wail or song over the dead.

XVI.

CORONACH.

He is gone on the mountain,
    He is lost to the forest,
Like a summer-dried fountain,
    When our need was the sorest.
The font, reappearing,
    From the raindrops shall borrow,
But to us comes no cheering,
    To Duncan no morrow !

The hand of the reaper
    Takes the ears that are hoary,
But the voice of the weeper
    Wails manhood in glory.
The autumn winds rushing
    Waft the leaves that are searest,
But our flower was in flushing,[1]
    When blighting was nearest.

Fleet foot on the correi,[2]
    Sage counsel in cumber,[3]
Red hand in the foray,
    How sound is thy slumber!
Like the dew on the mountain,
    Like the foam on the river,
Like the bubble on the fountain,
    Thou art gone, and forever!

XVII.

See Stumah,[4] who, the bier beside,
His master's corpse with wonder eyed,
Poor Stumah ! whom his least halloo

[1] Full bloom.   [2] The side of a hill which the game usually frequents.
[3] Trouble.   [4] The name of a dog.

Could send like lightning o'er the dew,
Bristles his crest, and points his ears,
As if some stranger step he hears.
'Tis not a mourner's muffled tread,
Who comes to sorrow o'er the dead,
But headlong haste, or deadly fear,
Urge the precipitate career.
All stand aghast: — unheeding all,
The henchman bursts into the hall;
Before the dead man's bier he stood;
Held forth the Cross besmear'd with blood:
"The muster-place is Lanrick mead;
Speed forth the signal! clansmen, speed!"

XVIII.

Angus, the heir of Duncan's line,
Sprung forth and seized the fatal sign.
In haste the stripling to his side
His father's dirk and broadsword tied;
But when he saw his mother's eye
Watch him in speechless agony,
Back to her open'd arms he flew,
Press'd on her lips a fond adieu —
"Alas!" she sobb'd, — "and yet, begone,
And speed thee forth, like Duncan's son!"
One look he cast upon the bier,
Dash'd from his eye the gathering tear,
Breathed deep to clear his laboring breast,
And toss'd aloft his bonnet crest,
Then, like the high-bred colt, when, freed,
First he essays his fire and speed,
He vanish'd, and o'er moor and moss
Sped forward with the Fiery Cross.
Suspended was the widow's tear,
While yet his footsteps she could hear;

And when she mark'd the henchman's eye
Wet with unwonted sympathy,
"Kinsman," she said, "his race is run,
That should have sped thine errand on;
The oak has fall'n,— the sapling bough
Is all Duncraggan's shelter now.
Yet trust I well, his duty done,
The orphan's God will guard my son.—
And you, in many a danger true,
At Duncan's hest[1] your blades that drew,
To arms, and guard that orphan's head !
Let babes and women wail the dead."
Then weapon clang, and martial call,
Resounded through the funeral hall,
While from the walls the attendant band
Snatch'd sword and targe, with hurried hand;
And short and flitting energy
Glanced from the mourner's sunken eye,
As if the sounds to warrior dear
Might rouse her Duncan from his bier.
But faded soon that borrow'd force;
Grief claim'd his right, and tears their course.

XIX.

Benledi saw the Cross of Fire,
It glanced like lightning up Strath-Ire.[2]
O'er dale and hill the summons flew,
Nor rest nor pause young Angus knew;
The tear that gather'd in his eye
He left the mountain breeze to dry;
Until, where Teith's young waters roll,
Betwixt him and a wooded knoll,
That graced the sable strath with green,
The chapel of St. Bride was seen.

---

[1] Behest; summons.   [2] The valley in which Loch Lubnaig lies.

Swoln was the stream, remote the bridge,
But Angus paused not on the edge;
Though the dark waves danced dizzily,
Though reel'd his sympathetic eye,
He dash'd amid the torrent's roar:
His right hand high the crosslet bore,
His left the poleax grasp'd, to guide
And stay his footing in the tide.
He stumbled twice — the foam splash'd high,
With hoarser swell the stream raced by;
And had he fall'n, — forever there,
Farewell Duncraggan's orphan heir!
But still, as if in parting life,
Firmer he grasp'd the Cross of strife,
Until the opposing bank he gain'd,
And up the chapel pathway strain'd.

XX.

A blithesome rout, that morning tide,[1]
Had sought the chapel of St. Bride.
Her troth Tombea's[2] Mary gave
To Norman, heir of Armandave,[2]
And, issuing from the Gothic arch,
The bridal[3] now resumed their march.
In rude, but glad procession, came
Bonneted sire and coif-clad dame;
And plaided youth, with jest and jeer,
Which snooded maiden would not hear;
And children, that, unwitting[4] why,
Lent the gay shout their shrilly cry;
And minstrels, that in measures vied
Before the young and bonny bride,

---

1 **Season.**   2 Tombea and Armandave are names of neighboring farmsteads.
3 Those composing the bridal procession.   4 Not knowing.

Whose downcast eye and cheek disclose
The tear and blush of morning rose.
With virgin step, and bashful hand,
She held the kerchief's snowy band;
The gallant bridegroom, by her side,
Beheld his prize with victor's pride,
And the glad mother in her ear
Was closely whispering word of cheer.

XXI.

Who meets them at the churchyard gate?
The messenger of fear and fate!
Haste in his hurried accent lies,
And grief is swimming in his eyes.
All dripping from the recent flood,
Panting and travel-soil'd he stood,
The fatal sign of fire and sword
Held forth, and spoke the appointed word:
"The muster-place is Lanrick mead —
Speed forth the signal! Norman, speed!"
And must he change so soon the hand,
Just link'd to his by holy band,
For the fell Cross of blood and brand?
And must the day, so blithe that rose,
And promised rapture in the close,
Before its setting hour, divide
The bridegroom from the plighted bride?
O fatal doom! — it must! it must!
Clan-Alpine's cause, her Chieftain's trust,
Her summons dread, brook no delay;
Stretch to the race — away! away!

XXII.

Yet slow he laid his plaid aside,
And, lingering, eyed his lovely bride,

Until he saw the starting tear
Speak woe he might not stop to cheer;
Then, trusting not a second look,
In haste he sped him up the brook,
Nor backward glanced, till on the heath
Where Lubnaig's lake supplies the Teith.
— What in the racer's bosom stirr'd ?
The sickening pang of hope deferr'd,
And memory, with a torturing train
Of all his morning visions vain.
Mingled with love's impatience, came
The manly thirst for martial fame ;
The stormy joy of mountaineers,
Ere yet they rush upon the spears ;
And zeal for Clan and Chieftain burning,
And hope, from well-fought field returning,
With war's red honors on his crest,
To clasp his Mary to his breast.
Stung by such thoughts, o'er bank and brae,
Like fire from flint he glanced away,
While high resolve, and feeling strong,
Burst into voluntary song.

XXIII.

SONG.

The heath this night must be my bed,
The bracken curtain for my head,
My lullaby the warder's tread,
    Far, far from love and thee, Mary;
To-morrow eve, more stilly laid,
My couch may be my bloody plaid,
My vesper song thy wail, sweet maid!
    It will not waken me, Mary!

I may not, dare not, fancy now
The grief that clouds thy lovely brow;
I dare not think upon thy vow,
    And all it promised me, Mary.
No fond regret must Norman know;
When bursts Clan-Alpine on the foe,
His heart must be like bended bow,
    His foot like arrow free, Mary.

A time will come with feeling fraught,
For, if I fall in battle fought,
Thy hapless lover's dying thought
    Shall be a thought of thee, Mary.
And if return'd from conquer'd foes,
How blithely will the evening close,
How sweet the linnet sing repose,
    To my young bride and me, Mary!

XXIV.

Not faster o'er thy heathery braes,
Balquhidder, speeds the midnight blaze,[1]
Rushing, in conflagration strong,
Thy deep ravines and dells along,
Wrapping thy cliffs in purple glow,
And reddening the dark lakes below;
Nor faster speeds it, nor so far,
As o'er thy heaths the voice of war.
The signal roused to martial coil[2]
The sullen margin of Loch Voil,
Waked still Loch Doine, and to the source
Alarm'd, Balvaig, thy swampy course;
Thence southward turn'd its rapid road

---

[1] Blaze of the heather, which is often set on fire by the shepherds to facilitate a growth of young herbage for the sheep.   [2] Noise; bustle.

Adown Strath-Gartney's valley broad,
Till rose in arms each man might claim
A portion in Clan-Alpine's name,
From the gray sire, whose trembling hand
Could hardly buckle on his brand,
To the raw boy, whose shaft and bow
Were yet scarce terror to the crow.
Each valley, each sequester'd glen,
Muster'd its little horde of men,
That met as torrents from the height
In Highland dales their streams unite,
Still gathering, as they pour along,
A voice more loud, a tide more strong,
Till at the rendezvous they stood
By hundreds prompt for blows and blood:
Each train'd to arms since life began,
Owning no tie but to his clan,
No oath, but by his Chieftain's hand,
No law, but Roderick Dhu's command.

XXV.

That summer morn had Roderick Dhu
Survey'd the skirts of Benvenue,
And sent his scouts o'er hill and heath,
To view the frontiers of Menteith.
All backward came with news of truce;
Still lay each martial Græme [1] and Bruce,[1]
In Rednock [2] courts no horsemen wait,
No banner waved on Cardross [2] gate,
On Duchray's [2] towers no beacon shone,
Nor scared the herons from Loch Con;
All seemed at peace. — Now wot ye why
The Chieftain, with such anxious eye,

---

[1] A powerful Lowland family (see Note 1, p. 52).
[2] A castle in the Forth valley (see map, p. 2).

Ere to the muster he repair,
This western frontier scann'd with care?—
In Benvenue's most darksome cleft,
A fair, though cruel, pledge was left;
For Douglas, to his promise true,
That morning from the isle withdrew,
And in a deep sequester'd dell
Had sought a low and lonely cell.
By many a bard, in Celtic tongue,
Has Coir-nan-Uriskin [1] been sung;
A softer name the Saxons gave,
And called the grot the Goblin-cave.

XXVI.

It was a wild and strange retreat,
As e'er was trod by outlaw's feet.
The dell, upon the mountain's crest,
Yawn'd like a gash on warrior's breast;
Its trench had stayed full many a rock,
Hurl'd by primeval earthquake shock
From Benvenue's gray summit wild,
And here, in random ruin piled,
They frown'd incumbent o'er the spot,
And form'd the rugged silvan grot.
The oak and birch, with mingled shade,
At noontide there a twilight made,
Unless when short and sudden shone
Some straggling beam on cliff or stone,
With such a glimpse as prophet's eye
Gains on thy depth, Futurity.
No murmur waked the solemn still,[2]
Save tinkling of a fountain rill;
But when the wind chafed with the lake,
A sullen sound would upward break,

---

[1] See Note 1, p. 87.   [2] Stillness.

With dashing hollow voice, that spoke
The incessant war of wave and rock.
Suspended cliffs, with hideous sway,
Seem'd nodding o'er the cavern gray.
From such a den the wolf had sprung,
In such the wild-cat leaves her young;
Yet Douglas and his daughter fair
Sought for a space their safety there.
Gray Superstition's whisper dread
Debarr'd the spot to vulgar tread;
For there, she said, did fays resort,
And satyrs [1] hold their silvan court,
By moonlight tread their mystic maze,
And blast the rash beholder's gaze.

XXVII.

Now eve, with western shadows long,
Floated on Katrine bright and strong,
When Roderick, with a chosen few,
Repass'd the heights of Benvenue.
Above the Goblin-cave they go,
Through the wild pass of Beal-nam-bo:
The prompt retainers speed before,
To launch the shallop from the shore,
For 'cross Loch Katrine lies his way
To view the passes of Achray,
And place his clansmen in array.
Yet lags the Chief in musing mind,
Unwonted sight, his men behind.
A single page, to bear his sword,
Alone attended on his lord;
The rest their way through thickets break,
And soon await him by the lake.

[1] Silvan deities of Greek mythology, with head and body of a man and legs
of a goat.

It was a fair and gallant sight,
To view them from the neighboring height,
By the low-level'd sunbeam's light!
For strength and stature, from the clan
Each warrior was a chosen man,
As even afar might well be seen,
By their proud step and martial mien.
Their feathers dance, their tartans float,
Their targets gleam, as by the boat
A wild and warlike group they stand,
That well became such mountain strand.

XXVIII.

Their Chief, with step reluctant, still
Was lingering on the craggy hill,
Hard by where turn'd apart the road
To Douglas's obscure abode.
It was but with that dawning morn,
That Roderick Dhu had proudly sworn
To drown his love in war's wild roar,
Nor think of Ellen Douglas more;
But he who stems [1] a stream with sand,
And fetters flame with flaxen band,
Has yet a harder task to prove —
By firm resolve to conquer love!
Eve finds the Chief, like restless ghost,
Still hovering near his treasure lost;
For though his haughty heart deny
A parting meeting to his eye,
Still fondly strains his anxious ear,
The accents of her voice to hear,
And inly did he curse the breeze
That waked to sound the rustling trees.

---

[1] Stops; checks.

But hark! what mingles in the strain?
It is the harp of Allan-Bane,
That wakes its measure slow and high,
Attuned to sacred minstrelsy.
What melting voice attends the strings?
'Tis Ellen, or an angel, sings.

XXIX.

HYMN TO THE VIRGIN.

Ave Maria! [1] maiden mild!
  Listen to a maiden's prayer!
Thou canst hear though from the wild,
  Thou canst save amid despair.
Safe may we sleep beneath thy care,
  Though banish'd, outcast, and reviled —
Maiden! hear a maiden's prayer!
  Mother, hear a suppliant child!
                              Ave Maria!

Ave Maria! undefiled!
  The flinty couch we now must share
Shall seem with down of eider [2] piled,
  If thy protection hover there.
The murky cavern's heavy air
  Shall breathe of balm if thou hast smiled·
Then, Maiden! hear a maiden's prayer!
  Mother, list a suppliant child!
                              Ave Maria!

Ave Maria! stainless styled!
  Foul demons of the earth and air,

---

[1] Hail, Mary! The beginning of the Roman Catholic prayer to the Virgin Mary.

[2] "Down of eider," i.e., the soft breast feathers of the eider duck.

From this their wonted haunt exiled,
  Shall flee before thy presence fair.
We bow us to our lot of care,
  Beneath thy guidance reconciled;
Hear for a maid a maiden's prayer!
  And for a father hear a child!
                              Ave Maria!

XXX.

Died on the harp the closing hymn. —
Unmoved in attitude and limb,
As list'ning still, Clan-Alpine's lord
Stood leaning on his heavy sword,
Until the page, with humble sign,
Twice pointed to the sun's decline.
Then while his plaid he round him cast,
"It is the last time — 'tis the last,"
He mutter'd thrice, — "the last time e'er
That angel voice shall Roderick hear!"
It was a goading thought — his stride
Hied hastier down the mountain side;
Sullen he flung him in the boat,
And instant 'cross the lake it shot.
They landed in that silvery bay,
And eastward held their hasty way,
Till, with the latest beams of light,
The band arrived on Lanrick height,
Where muster'd, in the vale below,
Clan-Alpine's men in martial show.

XXXI.

A various scene the clansmen made;
Some sate, some stood, some slowly stray'd;
But most, with mantles folded round,
Were couch'd to rest upon the ground,

Scarce to be known by curious eye,
From the deep heather where they lie,
So well was match'd the tartan screen
With heath bell dark and brackens green;
Unless where, here and there, a blade,
Or lance's point, a glimmer made,
Like glowworm twinkling through the shade.
But when, advancing through the gloom,
They saw the Chieftain's eagle plume,
Their shout of welcome, shrill and wide,
Shook the steep mountain's steady side.
Thrice it arose, and lake and fell
Three times return'd the martial yell;
It died upon Bochastle's plain,
And Silence claim'd her evening reign.

CANTO FOURTH.

THE PROPHECY.

I.

"THE rose is fairest when 'tis budding new,
      And hope is brightest when it dawns from fears;
The rose is sweetest wash'd with morning dew,
      And love is loveliest when embalm'd in tears.
O wilding[1] rose, whom fancy thus endears,
      I bid your blossoms in my bonnet wave,
Emblem of hope and love through future years !"—
      Thus spoke young Norman, heir of Armandave,
What time the sun arose on Vennachar's broad wave.

1 Wild.

II.

Such fond conceit, half said, half sung,
Love prompted to the bridegroom's tongue,
All while he stripp'd the wild-rose spray.
His ax and bow beside him lay,
For on a pass 'twixt lake and wood,
A wakeful sentinel he stood.
Hark! on the rock a footstep rung,
And instant to his arms he sprung.
"Stand, or thou diest !— What, Malise?— soon
Art thou return'd from Braes of Doune.
By thy keen step and glance I know,
Thou bring'st us tidings of the foe."—
(For while the Fiery Cross hied on,
On distant scout had Malise gone.)
"Where sleeps the Chief ?" the henchman said.-
"Apart, in yonder misty glade ;
To his lone couch I'll be your guide."—
Then call'd a slumberer by his side,
And stirr'd him with his slacken'd bow —
"Up, up, Glentarkin! rouse thee, ho !
We seek the Chieftain ; on the track,
Keep eagle watch till I come back."

III.

Together up the pass they sped:
"What of the foemen ?" Norman said. —
"Varying reports from near and far ;
This certain, — that a band of war
Has for two days been ready boune,[1]
At prompt command, to march from Doune ;
King James, the while, with princely powers,

---

[1] "Boune" itself means "ready" in Scotch: hence its use here is tautology.

Holds revelry in Stirling towers.
Soon will this dark and gathering cloud
Speak on our glens in thunder loud.
Inured to bide such bitter bout,
The warrior's plaid may bear it out;[1]
But, Norman, how wilt thou provide
A shelter for thy bonny bride?"—
"What! know ye not that Roderick's care
To the lone isle hath caused repair
Each maid and matron of the clan,
And every child and aged man
Unfit for arms; and given his charge,[2]
Nor skiff nor shallop, boat nor barge,
Upon these lakes shall float at large,
But all beside the islet moor,
That such dear pledge may rest secure?"—

IV.

"'Tis well advised — the Chieftain's plan
Bespeaks the father of his clan.
But wherefore sleeps Sir Roderick Dhu
Apart from all his followers true?"—
"It is, because last evening-tide
Brian an augury hath tried,
Of that dread kind which must not be
Unless in dread extremity;
The Taghairm[3] call'd; by which, afar,

---

[1] "Inured to bide," etc., i.e., accustomed to endure privations, the warrior may withstand the coming storm.   [2] Command; order.

[3] An old Highland mode of "reading the future." "A person was wrapped up in the skin of a newly slain bullock, and deposited beside a waterfall, or at the bottom of a precipice, or in some other strange, wild, and unusual situation. In this situation he revolved in his mind the question proposed, and whatever was impressed upon him by his exalted imagination passed for the inspiration of the disembodied spirits who haunt the desolate recesses."— *Scott.*

Our sires foresaw the events of war.
Duncraggan's milk-white bull they slew."

MALISE.

"Ah! well the gallant brute I knew!
The choicest of the prey we had,
When swept our merry men Gallangad.[1]
His hide was snow, his horns were dark,
His red eye glow'd like fiery spark;
So fierce, so tameless, and so fleet,
Sore did he cumber our retreat,
And kept our stoutest kernes [2] in awe,
Even at the pass of Beal 'maha.
But steep and flinty was the road,
And sharp the hurrying pikeman's goad,
And when we came to Dennan's Row,
A child might scathless [3] stroke his brow."

V.

NORMAN.

"That bull was slain: his reeking hide
They stretch'd the cataract beside,
Whose waters their wild tumult toss
Adown the black and craggy boss
Of that huge cliff, whose ample verge
Tradition calls the Hero's Targe.
Couch'd on a shelve beneath its brink,
Close where the thundering torrents sink,
Rocking beneath their headlong sway,
And drizzled by the ceaseless spray,
Midst groan of rock, and roar of stream,
The wizard waits prophetic dream.

---

[1] South of Loch Lomond.   [2] Foot soldiers.   [3] Without injury.

Nor distant rests the Chief; — but hush !
See, gliding slow through mist and bush,
The Hermit gains yon rock, and stands
To gaze upon our slumbering bands.
Seems he not, Malise, like a ghost,
That hovers o'er a slaughter'd host ?
Or raven on the blasted oak,
That, watching while the deer is broke,[1]
His morsel claims with sullen croak ? "

MALISE.

—" Peace ! peace ! to other than to me,
Thy words were evil augury;
But still I hold Sir Roderick's blade
Clan-Alpine's omen and her aid,
Not aught that, glean'd from heaven or hell,
Yon fiend-begotten monk can tell.
The Chieftain joins him, see — and now,
Together they descend the brow."

VI.

And, as they came, with Alpine's lord
The Hermit Monk held solemn word: —
" Roderick ! it is a fearful strife,
For man endowed with mortal life,
Whose shroud of sentient clay can still
Feel feverish pang and fainting chill,
Whose eye can stare in stony trance,
Whose hair can rouse like warrior's lance,—
'Tis hard for such to view, unfurl'd,
The curtain of the future world.
Yet, witness every quaking limb,
My sunken pulse, my eyeballs dim.

1 Cut up.

My soul with harrowing anguish torn,
This for my Chieftain have I borne !—
The shapes that sought my fearful couch,
A human tongue may ne'er avouch ;
No mortal man,— save he, who, bred
Between the living and the dead,
Is gifted beyond nature's law,—
Had e'er survived to say he saw.
At length the fateful answer came,
In characters of living flame !
Not spoke in word, nor blazed [1] in scroll,
But borne and branded on my soul ;—
WHICH SPILLS THE FOREMOST FOEMAN'S LIFE,
THAT PARTY CONQUERS IN THE STRIFE."—

VII.

"Thanks, Brian, for thy zeal and care !
Good is thine augury, and fair.
Clan-Alpine ne'er in battle stood,
But first our broadswords tasted blood.
A surer victim still I know,
Self-offer'd to the auspicious blow :
A spy has sought my land this morn,—
No eve shall witness his return !
My followers guard each pass's mouth,
To east, to westward, and to south ;
Red Murdoch, bribed to be his guide,
Has charge to lead his steps aside,
Till, in deep path or dingle brown,
He light on those shall bring him down.
—But see, who comes his news to show !
Malise ! what tidings of the foe ?"—

1 Emblazoned.

VIII.

"At Doune, o'er many a spear and glaive [1]
Two Barons proud their banners wave.
I saw the Moray's silver star,
And mark'd the sable pale [2] of Mar."—
"By Alpine's soul, high tidings those!
I love to hear of worthy foes.
When move they on?"—"To-morrow's noon
Will see them here for battle boune."—
"Then shall it see a meeting stern!—
But, for the place—say, couldst thou learn
Naught of the friendly clans of Earn? [3]
Strengthened by them, we well might bide
The battle on Benledi's side.
Thou couldst not?—Well! Clan-Alpine's men
Shall man the Trosachs' shaggy glen;
Within Loch Katrine's gorge we'll fight,
All in our maids' and matrons' sight,
Each for his hearth and household fire,
Father for child, and son for sire,
Lover for maid beloved!—But why—
Is it the breeze affects mine eye?
Or dost thou come, ill-omened tear!
A messenger of doubt or fear?
No! sooner may the Saxon lance
Unfix Benledi from his stance, [4]
Than doubt or terror can pierce through
The unyielding heart of Roderick Dhu!
'Tis stubborn as his trusty targe.
Each to his post—all know their charge."
The pibroch sounds, the bands advance,
The broadswords gleam, the banners dance,

---

[1] A sword.   [2] Black band in the coat of arms of the Earls of Mar.
[3] Loch Earn region.   [4] Foundation.

Obedient to the Chieftain's glance.
— I turn me from the martial roar,
And seek Coir-Uriskin once more.

IX.

Where is the Douglas? — he is gone;
And Ellen sits on the gray stone
Fast by the cave, and makes her moan;
While vainly Allan's words of cheer
Are pour'd on her unheeding ear.—
" He will return — Dear lady, trust !—
With joy return; — he will — he must.
Well was it time to seek, afar,
Some refuge from impending war,
When e'en Clan-Alpine's rugged swarm
Are cow'd by the approaching storm.
I saw their boats, with many a light,
Floating the livelong yesternight,
Shifting like flashes darted forth
By the red streamers of the north; [1]
I mark'd at morn how close they ride,
Thick moor'd by the lone islet's side,
Like wild ducks couching in the fen,
When stoops the hawk upon the glen.
Since this rude race dare not abide
The peril on the mainland side,
Shall not thy noble father's care
Some safe retreat for thee prepare ? "—

X.

ELLEN.

" No, Allan, no !   Pretext so kind
My wakeful terrors could not blind.

---

[1] " Red streamers," etc., i.e., the aurora borealis.

When in such tender tone, yet grave,
Douglas a parting blessing gave,
The tear that glisten'd in his eye
Drown'd not his purpose fix'd and high.
My soul, though feminine and weak,
Can image his; e'en as the lake,
Itself disturb'd by slightest stroke,
Reflects the invulnerable rock.
He hears report of battle rife,
He deems himself the cause of strife.
I saw him redden, when the theme
Turn'd, Allan, on thine idle dream
Of Malcolm Græme in fetters bound,
Which I, thou saidst, about him wound.
Think'st thou he trow'd [1] thine omen aught?
Oh no! 'twas apprehensive thought
For the kind youth,—for Roderick too—
(Let me be just) that friend so true;
In danger both, and in our cause!
Minstrel, the Douglas dare not pause.
Why else that solemn warning given,
'If not on earth, we meet in heaven?'
Why else, to Cambus-kenneth's fane,[2]
If eve return him not again,
Am I to hie, and make me known?
Alas! he goes to Scotland's throne,
Buys his friend's safety with his own;
He goes to do—what I had done,
Had Douglas' daughter been his son!"—

XI.

" Nay, lovely Ellen!—dearest, nay!
If aught should his return delay,

---

[1] Trusted.   [2] An abbey or church. This abbey is not far from Stirling.

Still Alice has her own Richard,
    And he his Alice Brand."

XIII.

BALLAD CONTINUED.

'Tis merry, 'tis merry, in good greenwood,
    So blithe Lady Alice is singing;
On the beech's pride, and oak's brown side,
    Lord Richard's ax is ringing.

Up spoke the moody Elfin King,
    Who won'd [1] within the hill, —
Like wind in the porch of a ruin'd church,
    His voice was ghostly shrill.

"Why sounds yon stroke on beech and oak,
    Our moonlight circle's screen?
Or who comes here to chase the deer,
    Beloved of our Elfin Queen?
Or who may dare on wold to wear
    The fairies' fatal green!

"Up, Urgan, up! to yon mortal hie,
    For thou wert christen'd man;
For cross or sign thou wilt not fly,
    For mutter'd word or ban.

"Lay on him the curse of the wither'd heart,
    The curse of the sleepless eye;
Till he wish and pray that his life would part,
    Nor yet find leave to die."

[1] Dwelt.

XIV.

BALLAD CONTINUED.

'Tis merry, 'tis merry, in good greenwood,
　　Though the birds have still'd their singing!
The evening blaze doth Alice raise,
　　And Richard is fagots bringing.

Up Urgan starts, that hideous dwarf,
　　Before Lord Richard stands,
And, as he cross'd and bless'd himself,
" I fear not sign," quoth the grisly elf,
　　" That is made with bloody hands."

But out then spoke she, Alice Brand,
　　That woman void of fear,—
"And if there's blood upon his hand,
　　'Tis but the blood of deer."—

" Now loud thou liest, thou bold of mood !
　　It cleaves unto his hand,
The stain of thine own kindly [1] blood,
　　The blood of Ethert Brand."

Then forward stepp'd she, Alice Brand,
　　And made the holy sign,—
"And if there's blood on Richard's hand,
　　A spotless hand is mine.

"And I conjure thee, demon elf,
　　By Him whom demons fear,
To show us whence thou art thyself,
　　And what thine errand here ?"

[1] Kindred.

XV.

BALLAD CONTINUED.

"'Tis merry, 'tis merry, in Fairyland,
   When fairy birds are singing,
When the court doth ride by their monarch's side,
   With bit and bridle ringing:

"And gayly shines the Fairyland —
   But all is glistening show,
Like the idle gleam that December's beam
   Can dart on ice and snow.

"And fading, like that varied gleam,
   Is our inconstant shape,
Who now like knight and lady seem,
   And now like dwarf and ape.

"It was between the night and day,
   When the Fairy King has power,
That I sunk down in a sinful fray,
And, 'twixt life and death, was snatched away
   To the joyless Elfin bower.

"But wist [1] I of a woman bold,
   Who thrice my brow durst sign,
I might regain my mortal mold,
   As fair a form as thine."

She cross'd him once — she cross'd him twice —
   That lady was so brave;
The fouler grew his goblin hue,
   The darker grew the cave.

[1] Knew.

She cross'd him thrice, that lady bold;
   He rose beneath her hand
The fairest knight on Scottish mold,
   Her brother, Ethert Brand!

Merry it is in good greenwood,
   When the mavis and merle are singing,
But merrier were they in Dunfermline [1] gray,
   When all the bells were ringing.

XVI.

Just as the minstrel sounds were stayed,
A stranger climb'd the steepy glade;
His martial step, his stately mien,
His hunting suit of Lincoln green,
His eagle glance, remembrance claims —
'Tis Snowdoun's Knight, 'tis James Fitz-James.
Ellen beheld as in a dream,
Then, starting, scarce suppress'd a scream:
"O stranger! in such hour of fear,
What evil hap has brought thee here?" —
"An evil hap how can it be,
That bids me look again on thee?
By promise bound, my former guide
Met me betimes this morning tide,
And marshal'd, over bank and bourne,[2]
The happy path of my return." —
"The happy path! — what! said he naught
Of war, of battle to be fought,
Of guarded pass?" — "No, by my faith!
Nor saw I aught could augur scathe."[3] —

---

[1] A town in Fifeshire, thirteen miles northwest of Edinburgh, the residence of the early Scottish kings. Its Abbey of the Gray Friars was the royal burial place.   [2] Boundary; stream.   [3] Harm.

"Oh haste thee, Allan, to the kern,[1]
— Yonder his tartans I discern;
Learn thou his purpose, and conjure
That he will guide the stranger sure! —
What prompted thee, unhappy man?
The meanest serf in Roderick's clan
Had not been bribed by love or fear,
Unknown to him to guide thee here."

XVII.

"Sweet Ellen, dear my life must be,
Since it is worthy care frôm thee;
Yet life I hold but idle breath,
When love or honor's weigh'd with death.
Then let me profit by my chance,
And speak my purpose bold at once.
I come to bear thee from a wild,
Where ne'er before such blossom smiled;
By this soft hand to lead thee far
From frantic scenes of feud and war.
Near Bochastle my horses wait;
They bear us soon to Stirling gate.
I'll place thee in a lovely bower,
I'll guard thee like a tender flower" —
"Oh! hush, Sir Knight! 'twere female art,
To say I do not read thy heart;
Too much, before, my selfish ear
Was idly soothed my praise to hear.
That fatal bait hath lured thee back,
In deathful hour, o'er dangerous track;
And how, oh how, can I atone
The wreck my vanity brought on! —

---

[1] Foot soldier.   Referring to the treacherous guide, Red Murdoch (see stanza VII. p. 109).

One way remains — I'll tell him all —
Yes ! struggling bosom, forth it shall !
Thou, whose light folly bears the blame
Buy thine own pardon with thy shame !
But first — my father is a man
Outlaw'd and exiled, under ban ;
The price of blood is on his head,
With me 'twere infamy to wed. —
Still wouldst thou speak? — then hear the truth !
Fitz-James, there is a noble youth, —
If yet he is ! — exposed for me
And mine to dread extremity [1] —
Thou hast the secret of my heart ;
Forgive, be generous, and depart ! "

XVIII.

Fitz-James knew every wily train [2]
A lady's fickle heart to gain ;
But here he knew and felt them vain.
There shot no glance from Ellen's eye,
To give her steadfast speech the lie ;
In maiden confidence she stood,
Though mantled in her cheek the blood,
And told her love with such a sigh
Of deep and hopeless agony,
As [3] death had seal'd her Malcolm's doom,
And she sat sorrowing on his tomb.
Hope vanish'd from Fitz-James's eye,
But not with hope fled sympathy.
He proffer'd to attend her side,
As brother would a sister guide. —
" Oh ! little know'st thou Roderick's heart !
Safer for both we go apart.

---

[1] Danger.   [2] Artifice.   [3] As if.

Oh haste thee, and from Allan learn,
If thou mayst trust yon wily kern."
With hand upon his forehead laid,
The conflict of his mind to shade,
A parting step or two he made;
Then, as some thought had cross'd his brain,
He paused, and turn'd, and came again.

XIX.

"Hear, lady, yet, a parting word !—
It chanced in fight that my poor sword
Preserved the life of Scotland's lord.
This ring the grateful Monarch gave,
And bade, when I had boon to crave,
To bring it back, and boldly claim
The recompense that I would name.
Ellen, I am no courtly lord,
But one who lives by lance and sword,
Whose castle is his helm and shield,
His lordship the embattled field.
What from a prince can I demand,
Who neither reck [1] of state nor land ?
Ellen, thy hand — the ring is thine ;
Each guard and usher knows the sign.
Seek thou the King without delay ;
This signet shall secure thy way ;
And claim thy suit, whate'er it be,
As ransom of his pledge to me."
He placed the golden circlet on,
Paused — kiss'd her hand — and then was gone.
The aged Minstrel stood aghast,
So hastily Fitz-James shot past.
He join'd his guide, and wending down

[1] Take heed.

The ridges of the mountain brown,
Across the stream they took their way,
That joins Loch Katrine to Achray.

XX.

All in the Trosachs' glen was still,
Noontide was sleeping on the hill:
Sudden his guide whoop'd loud and high —
" Murdoch ! was that a signal cry ? " —
He stamm'd forth — " I shout to scare
Yon raven rom his dainty fare."
He look'd — he knew the raven's prey,
His own br   e steed : — " Ah ! gallant gray !
For thee — f r me, perchance — 'twere well
We ne'er had een the Trosachs' dell. —
Murdoch, m   first — but silently ;
Whistle or wh   p, and thou shalt die ! "
Jealous and sullen, on they fared,
Each silent, each upon his guard.

XXI.

Now wound the path its dizzy ledge
Around a precipice's edge,
When lo ! a wasted female form,
Blighted by wrath of sun and storm,
In tatter'd weeds [1] and wild array,
Stood on a cliff beside the way,
And glancing round her restless eye,
Upon the wood, the rock, the sky,
Seem'd naught to mark, yet all to spy.
Her brow was wreath'd with gaudy broom ;
With gesture wild she waved a plume
Of feathers, which the eagles fling
To crag and cliff from dusky wing ;

---

[1] Garments.

Such spoils her desperate step had sought,
Where scarce was footing for the goat.
The tartan plaid she first descried,
And shriek'd till all the rocks replied;
As loud she laugh'd when near they drew,
For then the Lowland garb she knew;
And then her hands she wildly wrung,
And then she wept, and then she sung —
She sung! — the voice, in better time,
Perchance to harp or lute might chime;
And now, though strain'd and roughen'd, still
Rung wildly sweet to dale and hill.

XXII.

SONG.

They bid me sleep, they bid me pray,
   They say my brain is warp'd [1] and wrung —
I cannot sleep on Highland brae,
   I cannot pray in Highland tongue.
But were I now where Allan [2] glides,
Or heard my native Devan's [2] tides,
So sweetly would I rest, and pray
That Heaven would close my wintry day!

'Twas thus my hair they bade me braid,
   They made me to the church repair;
It was my bridal morn, they said,
   And my true love would meet me there.
But woe betide the cruel guile,
That drown'd in blood the morning smile!
And woe betide the fairy dream!
I only waked to sob and scream.

---

[1] Awry; confused.

[2] A beautiful stream which joins the Forth near Stirling.

XXIII.

"Who is this maid ? what means her lay ?
She hovers o'er the hollow way,
And flutters wide her mantle gray,
As the lone heron spreads his wing,
By twilight, o'er a haunted spring."—
"'Tis Blanche of Devan," Murdoch said,
"A crazed and captive Lowland maid,
Ta'en on the morn she was a bride,
When Roderick foray'd Devan-side;
The gay bridegroom resistance made,
And felt our Chief's unconquer'd blade.
I marvel she is now at large,
But oft she 'scapes from Maudlin's charge.—
Hence, brain-sick fool !"— He raised his bow:—
"Now, if thou strikest her but one blow,
I'll pitch thee from the cliff as far
As ever peasant pitch'd a bar !"[1]—
"Thanks, champion, thanks!" the maniac cried,
And press'd her to Fitz-James's side.
"See the gray pennons I prepare,
To seek my true love through the air !
I will not lend that savage groom,
To break his fall, one downy plume !
No !— deep amid disjointed stones,
The wolves shall batten[2] on his bones,
And then shall his detested plaid,
By bush and brier in mid air stayed,
Wave forth a banner fair and free,
Meet signal for their revelry."—

[1] " Pitching the bar " was a favorite athletic sport in Scotland.
[2] Fatten.

XXIV.

"Hush thee, poor maiden, and be still!"—
"Oh! thou look'st kindly, and I will.—
Mine eye has dried and wasted been,
But still it loves the Lincoln green;
And, though mine ear is all unstrung,
Still, still it loves the Lowland tongue.

"For oh my sweet William was forester true,
  He stole poor Blanche's heart away!
His coat it was all of the greenwood hue,
  And so blithely he trill'd the Lowland lay!

"It was not that I meant to tell . . .
But thou art wise, and guessest well."
Then, in a low and broken tone,
And hurried note, the song went on.
Still on the Clansman, fearfully,
She fixed her apprehensive eye;
Then turn'd it on the Knight, and then
Her look glanced wildly o'er the glen.

XXV.

"The toils are pitch'd, and the stakes are set,
  Ever sing merrily, merrily;
The bows they bend, and the knives they whet,
  Hunters live so cheerily.

"It was a stag, a stag of ten,[1]
  Bearing its branches sturdily;
He came stately down the glen,
  Ever sing hardily, hardily.

1 Having antlers with ten branches.

"It was there he met with a wounded doe,
    She was bleeding deathfully;
She warn'd him of the toils below,
    Oh, so faithfully, faithfully!

"He had an eye, and he could heed,
    Ever sing warily, warily;
He had a foot, and he could speed —
    Hunters watch so narrowly." [1]

XXVI.

Fitz-James's mind was passion-toss'd,
When Ellen's hints and fears were lost;
But Murdoch's shout suspicion wrought,
And Blanche's song conviction brought. —
Not like a stag that spies the snare,
But lion of the hunt aware,
He waved at once his blade on high,
"Disclose thy treachery, or die!"
Forth at full speed the Clansman flew,
But in his race his bow he drew.
The shaft just grazed Fitz-James's crest,
And thrill'd in Blanche's faded breast. —
Murdoch of Alpine! prove thy speed,
For ne'er had Alpine's son such need!
With heart of fire, and foot of wind,
The fierce avenger is behind!
Fate judges of the rapid strife —
The forfeit [2] death — the prize is life!
Thy kindred ambush lies before,
Close couch'd upon the heathery moor;

1 "The hunters are Clan-Alpine's men; the stag of ten is Fitz-James; the
wounded doe is herself!"—*Taylor.*   2 Penalty.

Them couldst thou reach !—it may not be—
Thine ambush'd kin thou ne'er shalt see,
The fiery Saxon gains on thee !
— Resistless speeds the deadly thrust,
As lightning strikes the pine to dust ;
With foot and hand Fitz-James must strain,
Ere he can win his blade again.
Bent o'er the fall'n, with falcon eye,
He grimly smiled to see him die ;
Then slower wended back his way
Where the poor maiden bleeding lay.

XXVII.

She sate beneath the birchen tree,
Her elbow resting on her knee ;
She had withdrawn the fatal shaft,
And gazed on it, and feebly laugh'd ;
Her wreath of broom and feathers gray,
Daggled [1] with blood, beside her lay.
The Knight to stanch the life-stream tried,—
"Stranger, it is in vain !" she cried.
"This hour of death has given me more
Of reason's power than years before ;
For, as these ebbing veins decay,
My frenzied visions fade away.
A helpless injured wretch I die,
And something tells me in thine eye,
That thou wert mine avenger born.—
Seest thou this tress ?—Oh ! still I've worn
This little tress of yellow hair,
Through danger, frenzy, and despair !
It once was bright and clear as thine,
But blood and tears have dimm'd its shine.

1 Wet.

I will not tell thee when 'twas shred,
Nor from what guiltless victim's head —
My brain would turn ! — but it shall wave
Like plumage on thy helmet brave,
Till sun and wind shall bleach the stain,
And thou wilt bring it me again. —
I waver still. — O God ! more bright
Let reason beam her parting light ! —
Oh! by thy knighthood's honor'd sign,
And for thy life preserved by mine,
When thou shalt see a darksome man,
Who boasts him Chief of Alpine's Clan,
With tartans broad, and shadowy plume,
And hand of blood, and brow of gloom,
Be thy heart bold, thy weapon strong,
And wreak [1] poor Blanche of Devan's wrong !
They watch for thee by pass and fell . . .
Avoid the path . . . O God ! . . . farewell."

XXVIII.

A kindly heart had brave Fitz-James;
Fast pour'd his eyes at pity's claims;
And now with mingled grief and ire,
He saw the murder'd maid expire.
" God, in my need, be my relief,
As I wreak this on yonder Chief !"
A lock from Blanche's tresses fair
He blended with her bridegroom's hair;
The mingled braid in blood he dyed,
And placed it on his bonnet-side:
" By Him whose word is truth ! I swear,
No other favor will I wear,
Till this sad token I imbrue

---

[1] Avenge.

In the best blood of Roderick Dhu.
— But hark ! what means yon faint halloo ?
The chase is up, — but they shall know,
The stag at bay's a dangerous foe."
Barr'd from the known but guarded way,
Through copse and cliffs Fitz-James must stray,
And oft must change his desperate track,
By stream and precipice turn'd back.
Heartless, fatigued, and faint, at length,
From lack of food and loss of strength,
He couch'd him in a thicket hoar,
And thought his toils and perils o'er : —
" Of all my rash adventures past,
This frantic feat must prove the last !
Who e'er so mad but might have guess'd,
That all this Highland hornet's nest
Would muster up in swarms so soon
As e'er they heard of bands [1] at Doune ?
Like bloodhounds now they search me out, —
Hark, to the whistle and the shout ! —
If farther through the wilds I go,
I only fall upon the foe :
I'll couch me here till evening gray,
Then darkling try my dangerous way."

XXIX.

The shades of eve come slowly down,
The woods are wrapt in deeper brown,
The owl awakens from her dell,
The fox is heard upon the fell ;
Enough remains of glimmering light
To guide the wanderer's steps aright,
Yet not enough from far to show

---

[1] Troops.

His figure to the watchful foe.
With cautious step, and ear awake,
He climbs the crag and threads the brake;
And not the summer solstice,[1] there,
Temper'd the midnight mountain air,
But every breeze, that swept the wold,
Benumb'd his drenched limbs with cold.
In dread, in danger, and alone,
Famish'd and chill'd, through ways unknown,
Tangled and steep, he journey'd on;
Till, as a rock's huge point he turn'd,
A watch fire close before him burn'd.

XXX.

Beside its embers red and clear,
Bask u, ... plaid, a mountaineer;
And up he sprung with sword in hand,—
"Thy name and purpose? Saxon, stand!"—
"A stranger."—"What dost thou require?"—
"Rest and a guide, and food and fire.
My life's beset, my path is lost,
The gale has chill'd my limbs with frost."—
"Art thou a friend to Roderick?"—"No."—
"Thou darest not call thyself a foe?"—
"I dare! to him and all the band
He brings to aid his murderous hand."—
"Bold words!—but, though the beast of game
The privilege of chase may claim,
Though space and law the stag we lend,
Ere hound we slip,[2] or bow we bend,
Who ever reck'd, where, how, or when,
The prowling fox was trapp'd or slain?
Thus treacherous scouts,—yet sure they lie,

---

[1] Midsummer heat.   [2] Loose from the leash.

Who say thou camest a secret spy !" —
" They do, by Heaven ! — Come Roderick Dhu,
And of his clan the boldest two,
And let me but till morning rest,
I write the falsehood on their crest." —
" If by the blaze I mark aright,
Thou bear'st the belt and spur of Knight." —
" Then by these tokens mayest thou know
Each proud oppressor's mortal foe." —
" Enough, enough ; — sit down, and share
A soldier's couch, a soldier's fare."

XXXI.

He gave him of his Highland cheer,
The harden'd flesh of mountain deer ;
Dry fuel on the fire he laid,
And bade the Saxon share his plaid.
He tended him like welcome guest,
Then thus his farther speech address'd : —
" Stranger, I am to Roderick Dhu
A clansman born, a kinsman true ;
Each word against his honor spoke,
Demands of me avenging stroke ;
Yet more, upon thy fate, 'tis said,
A mighty augury [1] is laid.
It rests with me to wind my horn, —
Thou art with numbers overborne ;
It rests with me, here, brand to brand,
Worn as thou art, to bid thee stand :
But, not for clan, nor kindred's cause,
Will I depart from honor's laws ;
To assail a wearied man were shame,
And stranger is a holy name ;

---

[1] See Stanza VI. p. 109.

Guidance and rest, and food and fire,
In vain he never must require.
Then rest thee here till dawn of day;
Myself will guide thee on the way,
O'er stock and stone, through watch and ward,
Till past Clan-Alpine's utmost guard,
As far as Coilantogle's ford;
From thence thy warrant [1] is thy sword."—
"I take thy courtesy, by Heaven,
As freely as 't nobly given!"—
"Well, rest thee; for the bittern's cry
Sings us the lake's wild lullaby."
With that he shook the gather'd heath,
And spread his plaid upon the wreath;
And the brave foemen, side by side,
Lay peaceful down, like brothers tried,
And slept until the dawning beam
Purpled the mountain and the stream.

CANTO FIFTH.

THE COMBAT.

I.

FAIR as the earliest beam of eastern light,
    When first, by the bewilder'd pilgrim spied,
It smiles upon the dreary brow of night,
    And silvers o'er the torrent's foaming tide,
And lights the fearful path on mountain side;—

[1] Safeguard.

Fair as that beam, although the fairest far,
 Giving to horror grace, to danger pride,
  Shine martial Faith, and Courtesy's bright star,
 Through all the wreckful storms that cloud the brow of War

II.

That early beam, so fair and sheen,
Was twinkling through the hazel screen,
When, rousing at its glimmer red,
The warriors left their lowly bed,
Look'd out upon the dappled sky,
Mutter'd their soldier matins by,
And then awaked their fire, to steal,[1]
As short and rude, their soldier meal.
That o'er, the Gael around him threw
His graceful plaid of varied hue,
And, true to promise, led the way,
By thicket green and mountain gray.
A wildering path! — they winded now
Along the precipice's brow,
Commanding the rich scenes beneath,
The windings of the Forth and Teith,
And all the vales beneath that lie,
Till Stirling's turrets melt in sky;
Then, sunk in copse, their farthest glance
Gain'd not the length of horseman's lance.
'Twas oft so steep, the foot was fain
Assistance from the hand to gain;
So tangled oft, that, bursting through,
Each hawthorn shed her showers of dew, —
That diamond dew, so pure and clear,
It rivals all but Beauty's tear!

---

[1] Eat hastily.

III.

At length they came where, stern and steep,
The hill sinks down upon the deep.
Here Vennachar in silver flows,
There, ridge on ridge, Benledi rose;
Ever the hollow path twined on,
Beneath steep bank and threatening stone;
An hundred men might hold the post
With hardihood against a host.
The rugged mountain's scanty cloak
Was dwarfish shrubs of birch and oak,
With shingles [1] bare, and cliffs between,
And patches bright of bracken green,
And heather black, that waved so high,
It held the copse in rivalry.
But where the lake slept deep and still,
Dank [2] osiers fringed the swamp and hill;
And oft both path and hill were torn,
Where wintry torrent down had borne,
And heap'd upon the cumber'd land
Its wreck of gravel, rocks, and sand.
So toilsome was the road to trace,
The guide, abating of his pace,
Led slowly through the pass's jaws,
And ask'd Fitz-James, by what strange cause
He sought these wilds, traversed by few,
Without a pass from Roderick Dhu.

IV.

" Brave Gael, my pass in danger tried,
Hangs in my belt, and by my side;
Yet, sooth to tell," the Saxon said,
" I dreamt not now to claim its aid.

---

[1] Pebbles.   [2] Moist.

When here, but three days since, I came,
Bewilder'd in pursuit of game,
All seem'd as peaceful and as still
As the mist slumbering on yon hill;
Thy dangerous Chief was then afar,
Nor soon expected back from war.
Thus said, at least, my mountain guide,
Though deep, perchance, the villain lied."—
"Yet why a second venture try?"—
"A warrior thou, and ask me why!—
Moves our free course by such fix'd cause
As gives the poor mechanic laws?
Enough, I sought to drive away
The lazy hours of peaceful day;
Slight cause will then suffice to guide
A Knight's free footsteps far and wide,—
A falcon flown, a greyhound stray'd,
The merry glance of mountain maid:
Or, if a path be dangerous known,
The danger's self is lure alone."—

v.

"Thy secret keep, I urge thee not;—
Yet, ere again ye sought this spot,
Say, heard ye naught of Lowland war,
Against Clan-Alpine, raised by Mar?"
— "No, by my word;— of bands prepared
To guard King James's sports I heard;
Nor doubt I aught, but, when they hear
This muster of the mountaineer,
Their pennons will abroad be flung,
Which else in Doune had peaceful hung."—
"Free be they flung!— for we were loth
Their silken folds should feast the moth.
Free be they flung!— as free shall wave

Clan-Alpine's pine in banner brave.
But, Stranger, peaceful since you came,
Bewilder'd in the mountain game,
Whence the bold boast by which you show[1]
Vich-Alpine's vow'd and mortal foe ? " —
" Warrior, but yester-morn, I knew
Naught of thy Chieftain, Roderick Dhu,
Save as an outlaw'd desperate man,
The chief of a rebellious clan,
Who, in the Regent's[2] court and sight,
With ruffian dagger stabb'd a knight:
Yet this alone might from his part
Sever each true and loyal heart."

VI.

Wrothful at such arraignment foul,
Dark lower'd the ......man's sable scowl.
A sp.......ie paused, then sternly said,
" And heardst thou why he drew his blade?
Heardst thou, that shameful word and blow
Brought Roderick's vengeance on his foe ?
What reck'd the Chieftain if he stood
On Highland heath, or Holy-Rood ?
He rights such wrong where it is given,
If it were in the court of heaven." —
" Still was it outrage ; — yet, 'tis true,
Not then claim'd sovereignty his due;
While Albany, with feeble hand,
Held borrow'd truncheon of command,
The young King, mew'd[3] in Stirling tower,
Was stranger to respect and power.[4]

---

[1] Declare yourself to be.

[2] Duke of Albany (see Introduction, p. 12, and Stanza VI.).

[3] Imprisoned.

[4] That period of Scottish history from the battle of Flodden to the major-
ity of James V. was full of disorder and violence.

But then, thy Chieftain's robber life !—
Winning mean prey by causeless strife,
Wrenching from ruin'd Lowland swain
His herds and harvest rear'd in vain. —
Methinks a soul, like thine, should scorn
The spoils from such foul foray borne."

VII.

The Gael beheld him grim the while,
And answer'd with disdainful smile,—
"Saxon, from yonder mountain high,
I mark'd thee send delighted eye,
Far to the south and east, where lay,
Extend'd in succession gay,
Deep waving fields and pastures green,
With gentle slope and groves between:—
These fertile plains, the soften'd vale,
Were once the birthright of the Gael;
The stranger came with iron hand,
And from our fathers reft [1] the land.
Where dwell we now?   See, rudely swell
Crag over crag, and fell o'er fell.
Ask we this savage hill we tread,
For fatten'd steer or household bread;
Ask we for flocks these shingles dry,—
And well the mountain might reply,
'To you, as to your sires of yore,
Belong the target and claymore !
I give you shelter in my breast,
Your own good blades must win the rest.'
Pent in this fortress of the north,
Thinkst thou we will not sally forth,
To spoil the spoiler as we may,
And from the robber rend the prey?

[1] Robbed.

Ay, by my soul !— While on yon plain
The Saxon rears one shock of grain;
While, of ten thousand herds, there strays
But one along yon river's maze, —
The Gael, of plain and river heir,
Shall, with strong hand, redeem his share.
Where live the mountain Chiefs who hold,
That plundering Lowland field and fold
Is aught but retribution true?
Seek other cause 'gainst Roderick Dhu." —

VIII.

Answer'd Fitz-James, — " And, if I sought,
Thinkst thou no other could be brought?
What deem ye of my path waylaid?
My life given o'er to ambuscade ? " —
"As of a meed to rashness due: ·
Hadst thou sent warning fair and true, —
I seek my hound, or falcon stray'd,
I seek good faith,[1] a Highland maid, —
Free hadst thou been to come and go;
But secret path marks secret foe.
Nor yet, for this, even as a spy,
Hadst thou, unheard, been doom'd to die,
Save to fulfill an augury."—
" Well, let it pass; nor will I now
Fresh cause of enmity avow,
To chafe thy mood and cloud thy brow.
Enough, I am by promise tied
To match me with this man of pride:
Twice have I sought Clan-Alpine's glen
In peace; but when I come agen,
I come with banner, brand, and bow,
As leader seeks his mortal foe.

---

[1] " Good faith," i.e., in good faith.

For lovelorn swain, in lady's bower,
Ne'er panted for the appointed hour,
As I, until before me stand
This rebel Chieftain and his band!"—

IX.

"Have, then, thy wish!"— He whistled shrill,
And he was answer'd from the hill;
Wild as the scream of the curlew,
From crag to crag the signal flew.
Instant, through copse and heath, arose
Bonnets and spears and bended bows;
On right, on left, above, below,
Sprung up at once the lurking foe;
From shingles gray their lances start,
The bracken bush sends forth the dart,
The rushes and the willow wand
Are bristling into ax and brand,
And every tuft of broom gives life
To plaided warrior arm'd for strife.
That whistle garrison'd the glen
At once with full five hundred men,
As if the yawning hill to heaven
A subterranean host had given.
Watching their leader's beck and will,
All silent there they stood, and still.
Like the loose crags, whose threatening mass
Lay tottering o'er the hollow pass,
As if an infant's touch could urge
Their headlong passage down the verge,
With step and weapon forward flung,
Upon the mountain side they hung.
The Mountaineer cast glance of pride
Along Benledi's living side,
Then fix'd his eye and sable brow

Full on Fitz-James — " How say'st thou now?
These are Clan-Alpine's warriors true;
And, Saxon, — I am Roderick Dhu!"

                              X.

Fitz-James was brave: — Though to his heart
The lifeblood thrill'd with sudden start,
He mann'd himself with dauntless air,
Return'd the Chief his haughty stare,
His back against a rock he bore,
And firmly placed his foot before: —
" Come one, come all ! this rock shall fly
From its firm base as sóon as I."
Sir Roderick mark'd — and in his eyes
Respect was mingled with surprise,
And the stern joy which warriors feel
In foemen worthy of their steel.
Short space he stood — then waved his hand
Down sunk the disappearing band;
Each warrior vanish'd where he stood,
In broom or bracken, heath or wood;
Sunk brand and spear and bended bow,
In osiers pale and copses low;
It seem'd as if their mother Earth
Had swallowed up her warlike birth.
The wind's last breath had toss'd in air
Pennon, and plaid, and plumage fair, —
The next but swept a lone hillside,
Where heath and fern were waving wide:
The sun's last glance was glinted [1] back,
From spear and glaive, from targe and jack,-
The next, all unreflected, shone
On bracken green, and cold gray stone.

                      [1] Flashed.

XI.

Fitz-James look'd round — yet scarce believed
The witness that his sight received;
Such apparition well might seem
Delusion of a dreadful dream.
Sir Roderick in suspense he eyed,
And to his look the Chief replied,
" Fear naught — nay, that I need not say —
But — doubt not aught from mine array.
Thou art my guest; — I pledged my word
As far as Coilantogle ford:
Nor would I call a clansman's brand
For aid against one valiant hand,
Though on our strife lay every vale
Rent by the Saxon from the Gael.
So move we on; — I only meant
To show the reed on which you leant,
Deeming this path you might pursue
Without a pass from Roderick Dhu."
They mov'd: — I said Fitz-James was brave,
As ever knight that belted glaive;
Yet dare not say, that now his blood
Kept on its wont and temper'd flood,[1]
As, following Roderick's stride, he drew
That seeming lonesome pathway through,
Which yet, by fearful proof, was rife
With lances, that, to take his life,
Waited but signal from a guide
So late dishonor'd and defied.
Ever, by stealth, his eye sought round
The vanish'd guardians of the ground,
And still, from copse and heather deep,
Fancy saw spear and broadsword peep,

---

[1] Flow.

And in the plover's shrilly strain,
The signal-whistle heard again.
Nor breathed he free till far behind
The pass was left; for then they wind
Along a wide and level green,
Where neither tree nor tuft was seen,
Nor rush nor bush of broom was near,
To hide a bonnet or a spear.

XII.

The Chief in silence strode before,
And reach'd that torrent's sounding shore,
Which, daughter of three mighty lakes,[1]
From Vennachar in silver breaks,
Sweeps through the plain, and ceaseless mines
On Bochastle the moldering lines,
Where Rome, the Empress of the world,
Of yore her eagle [2] wings unfurl'd.
And here his course the Chieftain stayed,
Threw down his target and his plaid,
And to the Lowland warrior said,—
"Bold Saxon! to his promise just,
Vich-Alpine has discharged his trust.
This murderous Chief, this ruthless man,
This head of a rebellious clan,
Hath led thee safe, through watch and ward,
Far past Clan-Alpine's outmost guard.
Now, man to man, and steel to steel,
A Chieftain's vengeance thou shalt feel.
See here, all vantageless [3] I stand,

---

[1] Katrine, Achray, and Vennachar.

[2] The eagle, with wings displayed and a thunderbolt in one of its talons, was the ensign of the Roman legions. Ancient earthworks near Bochastle are thought to date back to the Roman occupation of Britain.

[3] Without advantage.

Arm'd, like thyself, with single brand:
For this is Coilantogle ford,
And thou must keep thee with thy sword."

XIII.

The Saxon paused : — " I ne'er delay'd
When foeman bade me draw my blade ;
Nay, more, brave Chief, I vow'd thy death:
Yet sure thy fair and generous faith,
And my deep debt for life preserv'd,
A better meed have well deserv'd:
Can naught but blood our feud atone?
Are there no means ? " — " No, Stranger, none !
And hear, — to fire thy flagging zeal, —
The Saxon cause rests on thy steel ;
For thus spoke Fate, by prophet bred
Between the living and the dead:
'Who spills the foremost foeman's life,
His party conquers in the strife.' " —
" Then, by my word," the Saxon said,
" The riddle is already read.
Seek yonder brake beneath the cliff, —
There lies Red Murdoch, stark and stiff.
Thus Fate hath solved her prophecy,
Then yield to Fate, and not to me.
To James, at Stirling, let us go,
When, if thou wilt be still his foe,
Or if the King shall not agree
To grant thee grace and favor free,[1]
I plight mine honor, oath, and word,
That, to thy native strengths[2] restored,
With each advantage shalt thou stand,
That aids thee now to guard thy land."

---

[1] Complete.   [2] Strongholds.

XIV.

Dark lightning flash'd from Roderick's eye —
"Soars thy presumption, then, so high,
Because a wretched kern ye slew,
Homage to name to Roderick Dhu?
He yields not, he, to man nor Fate!
Thou add'st but fuel to my hate: —
My clansman's blood demands revenge.
Not yet prepared? — By Heaven, I change
My thought, and hold thy valor light
As that of some vain carpet knight,
Who ill deserved my courteous care,
And whose best boast is but to wear
A braid of his fair lady's hair." —
"I thank thee, Roderick, for the word!
It nerves my heart, it steels my sword;
For I have sworn this braid to stain
In the best blood that warms thy vein.
Now, truce, farewell! and, ruth, begone! —
Yet think not that by thee alone,
Proud Chief! can courtesy be shown;
Though not from copse, or heath, or cairn,
Start at my whistle clansmen stern,
Of this small horn one feeble blast
Would fearful odds against thee cast.
But fear not — doubt not — which thou wilt —
We try this quarrel hilt to hilt." —
Then each at once his falchion drew,
Each on the ground his scabbard threw,
Each look'd to sun, and stream, and plain,
As what they ne'er might see again;
Then foot, and point, and eye opposed,
In dubious strife they darkly closed.

XV.

Ill fared it then with Roderick Dhu,
That on the field his targe he threw,
Whose brazen studs and tough bull hide
Had death so often dash'd aside;
For, train'd abroad [1] his arms to wield,
Fitz-James's blade was sword and shield.
He practiced every pass and ward,
To thrust, to strike, to feint, to guard;
While less expert, though stronger far,
The Gael maintain'd unequal war.
Three times in closing strife they stood,
And thrice the Saxon blade drank blood;
No stinted draught, no scanty tide,
The gushing flood the tartans dyed.
Fierce Roderick felt the fatal drain,
And shower'd his blows like wintry rain;
And, as firm rock, or castle roof,
Against the winter shower is proof,
The foe, invulnerable still,
Foil'd his wild rage by steady skill;
Till, at advantage ta'en, his brand
Forced Roderick's weapon from his hand,
And backward borne upon the lea,
Brought the proud Chieftain to his knee.

XVI.

" Now, yield thee, or by Him who made
The world, thy heart's blood dyes my blade!"—
" Thy threats, thy mercy, I defy!
Let recreant yield, who fears to die."
— Like adder darting from his coil,
Like wolf that dashes through the toil,

---

[1] In France.

Like mountain cat who guards her young,
Full at Fitz-James's throat he sprung;
Received, but reck'd not of a wound,
And lock'd his arms his foeman round. —
Now, gallant Saxon, hold thine own!
No maiden's hand is round thee thrown!
That desperate grasp thy frame might feel,
Through bars of brass and triple steel! —
They tug, they strain! down, down they go,
The Gael above, Fitz-James below.
The Chieftain's gripe his throat compress'd,
His knee was planted in his breast;
His clotted locks he backward threw,
Across his brow his hand he drew,
  rom blood and mist to clear his sight,
 'hen gleam'd aloft his dagger bright! —
— 'ut hate and fury ill supplied
The . eam of life's exhausted tide,
And a. too late the advantage came,
To turn the odds of deadly game;
For, while the dagger gleam'd on high,
Reel'd soul and sense, reel'd brain and eye.
Down came the blow! but in the heath
The erring blade found bloodless sheath.
The struggling foe may now unclasp
The fainting Chief's relaxing grasp;
Unwounded from the dreadful close,
But breathless all, Fitz-James arose.

XVII.

He falter'd thanks to Heaven for life,
Redeem'd, unhoped, from desperate strife;
Next on his foe his look he cast,
Whose every gasp appear'd his last;
In Roderick's gore he dipt the braid, —

" Poor Blanche ! thy wrongs are dearly paid:
Yet with thy foe must die, or live,
The praise that Faith and Valor give."
With that he blew a bugle note,
Undid the collar from his throat,
Unbonneted, and by the wave
Sate down his brow and hands to lave.
Then faint afar are heard the feet
Of rushing steeds in gallop fleet;
The sounds increase, and now are seen
Four mounted squires in Lincoln green;
Two who bear lance, and two who lead,
By loosen'd rein, a saddled steed;
Each onward held his headlong course,
And by Fitz-James rein'd up his horse, —
With wonder view'd the bloody spot —
" Exclaim not, gallants ! question not. —
You, Herbert and Luffness, alight,
And bind the wounds of yonder knight;
Let the gray palfrey bear his weight,
We destined for a fairer freight,
And bring him on to Stirling straight;
I will before at better speed,
To seek fresh horse and fitting weed.
The sun rides high; — I must be boune,
To see the archer game at noon;
But lightly Bayard clears the lea. —
De Vaux and Herries, follow me.

XVIII.

" Stand, Bayard, stand !" — the steed obey'd,
With arching neck and bended head,
And glancing eye and quivering ear,
As if he loved his lord to hear.
No foot Fitz-James in stirrup stayed,

No grasp upon the saddle laid,
But wreath'd his left hand in the mane,
And lightly bounded from the plain,
Turn'd on the horse his armed heel,
And stirr'd his courage with the steel.[1]
Bounded the fiery steed in air,
The rider sate erect and fair,
Then like a bolt from steel crossbow
Forth launch'd, along the plain they go.
They dash'd that rapid torrent through,
And up Carhonie's [2] hill they flew;
Still at the gallop prick'd [3] the Knight,
His merry-men follow'd as they might.
Along thy banks, swift Teith! they ride,
And in the race they mock thy tide;
Torry and Lendrick now are past,
And Deanstown lies behind them cast;
They rise, the banner'd towers of Doune,
They sink in distant woodland soon;
Blair-Drummond sees the hoofs strike fire,
They sweep like breeze through Ochtertyre;
They mark just glance and disappear
The lofty brow of ancient Kier;
They bathe their coursers' sweltering sides,
Dark Forth! amid thy sluggish tides,
And on the opposing shore take ground,
With plash, with scramble, and with bound.
Right-hand they leave thy cliffs, Craig-Forth!
And soon the bulwark of the North,
Gray Stirling, with her towers and town,
Upon their fleet career look'd down.

[1] Spur.   [2] About a mile from the mouth of Lake Vennachar.
[3] Spurred.

XIX.

As up the flinty path they strain'd,
Sudden his steed the leader rein'd;
A signal to his squire he flung,
Who instant to his stirrup sprung: —
"Seest thou, De Vaux, yon woodsman gray,
Who townward holds the rocky way,
Of stature tall and poor array?
Mark'st thou the firm, yet active stride,
With which he scales the mountain side?
Know'st thou from whence he comes, or whom? —
"No, by my word; — a burly groom
He seems, who in the field or chase
A baron's train would nobly grace." —
"Out, out, De Vaux! can fear supply,
And jealousy, no sharper eye?
Afar, ere to the hill he drew,
That stately form and step I knew;
Like form in Scotland is not seen,
Treads not such step on Scottish green.
'Tis James of Douglas, by St. Serle!
The uncle of the banish'd Earl.
Away, away, to court, to show
The near approach of dreaded foe:
The King must stand upon his guard;
Douglas and he must meet prepared."
Then right-hand wheel'd their steeds, and straight
They won the Castle's postern gate.

XX.

The Douglas, who had bent his way
From Cambus-kenneth's Abbey gray,
Now, as he climb'd the rocky shelf,
Held sad communion with himself: —

"Yes! all is true my fears could frame;
A prisoner lies the noble Græme,
And fiery Roderick soon will feel
The vengeance of the royal steel.
I, only I, can ward their fate, —
God grant the ransom come not late!
The Abbess hath her promise given,
My child shall be the bride of Heaven;[1] —
— Be pardon'd one repining tear!
For He, who gave her, knows how dear,
How excellent! but that is by,
And now my business is — to die.
— Ye towers! within whose circuit dread
A Douglas[2] by his sovereign bled;
And thou, O sad and fatal mound![3]
That oft hast heard the death-ax sound,
As on the noblest of the land
Fell the stern headsman's bloody hand, —
The dungeon, block, and nameless tomb
Prepare — for Douglas seeks his doom! —
— But hark! what blithe and jolly peal
Makes the Franciscan[4] steeple reel?
And see! upon the crowded street,
In motley groups what maskers meet!
Banner and pageant, pipe and drum,
And merry morris dancers[5] come.
I guess, by all this quaint array,

1 "Bride of Heaven," i.e., a nun.

2 William, eighth earl of Douglas, was stabbed by James II. while in Stirling Castle, and under royal safe-conduct.

3 "Heading Hill," where executions took place.

4 A church of the Franciscans or Gray Friars was built near the castle, in 1494, by James IV.

5 The morris dance was of Moorish origin, and brought from Spain to England, where it was combined with the national Mayday games. The dress of the dancers was adorned with party-colored ribbons, and little bells were

The burghers hold their sports to-day.[1]
James will be there; he loves such show,
Where the good yeoman bends his bow,
And the tough wrestler foils his foe,
As well as where, in proud career,
The high-born tilter shivers spear.
I'll follow to the Castle-park,
And play my prize; — King James shall mark,
If age has tamed these sinews stark,[2]
Whose force so oft, in happier days,
His boyish wonder loved to praise."

XXI.

The Castle gates were open flung,
The quivering drawbridge rock'd and rung,
And echo'd loud the flinty street
Beneath the coursers' clattering feet,
As slowly down the steep descent
Fair Scotland's King and nobles went,
While all along the crowded way
Was jubilee and loud huzza.
And ever James was bending low,
To his white jennet's[3] saddlebow,
Doffing his cap to city dame,
Who smiled and blush'd for pride and shame.
And well the simperer might be vain, —
He chose the fairest of the train.
Gravely he greets each city sire,
Commends each pageant's quaint attire,
Gives to the dancers thanks aloud,

attached to their anklets, armlets, or girdles. The dancers often personated
various fictitious characters.

[1] Every borough had its solemn play or festival, where archery, wrestling,
hurling the bar, and other athletic exercises, were engaged in.

[2] Strong.   [3] A small Spanish horse.

And smiles and nods upon the crowd,
Who rend the heavens with their acclaims,—
" Long live the Commons' King,[1] King James !"
Behind the King throng'd peer and knight,
And noble dame, and damsel bright,
Whose fiery steeds ill brook'd the stay
Of the steep street and crowded way.
— But in the train you might discern
Dark lowering brow, and visage stern :
There nobles mourn'd their pride restrain'd,
And the mean burgher's joys disdain'd ;
And chiefs, who, hostage for their clan,
Were each from home a banish'd man,
There thought upon their own gray tower,
Their waving woods, their feudal power,
And deem'd themselves a shameful part
Of pageant which they cursed in heart.

XXII.

Now, in the Castle-park, drew out
Their checker'd [2] bands the joyous rout.
There morrisers, with bell at heel,
And blade in hand, their mazes wheel ;
But chief, beside the butts, there stand
Bold Robin Hood [3] and all his band,—
Friar Tuck [4] with quarterstaff and cowl,
Old Scathlock [4] with his surly scowl,

---

1 Like Henry VIII. in England, and Louis XI. in France, James V. had checked the lawless nobles, and favored the commons or burghers.

2 In clothing of varied form and color.

3 A renowned English outlaw and robber, supposed to have lived at the end of the twelfth and beginning of the thirteenth century, and to have frequented Sherwood Forest. Characters representing him and his followers were often introduced into the popular games.

4 Follower of Robin Hood.

Maid Marian,[1] fair as ivory bone,
Scarlet,[1] and Mutch,[1] and Little John;[1]
Their bugles challenge all that will,
In archery to prove their skill.
The Douglas bent a bow of might,—
His first shaft centered in the white,
And when in turn he shot again,
His second split the first in twain.
From the King's hand must Douglas take
A silver dart,[2] the archer's stake;
Fondly he watch'd, with watery eye,
Some answering glance of sympathy, —
No kind emotion made reply!
Indifferent as to archer wight,[3]
The Monarch gave the arrow bright.

XXIII.

Now, clear the ring! for, hand to hand,
The manly wrestlers take their stand.
Two o'er the rest superior rose,
And proud demanded mightier foes,
Nor call'd in vain; for Douglas came.
— For life is Hugh of Larbert lame;
Scarce better John of Alloa's fare,
Whom senseless home his comrades bear.
Prize of the wrestling match, the King
To Douglas gave a golden ring,
While coldly glanced his eye of blue,
As frozen drop of wintry dew.
Douglas would speak, but in his breast
His struggling soul his words suppress'd;
Indignant then he turn'd him where

---

[1] Follower of Robin Hood.
[2] The usual prize to the best shooter was a silver arrow.
[3] A simple, ordinary archer.

Their arms the brawny yeoman bare,
To hurl the massive bar in air.
When each his utmost strength had shown,
The Douglas rent an earth-fast stone
From its deep bed, then heaved it high,
And sent the fragment through the sky,
A rood beyond the farthest mark; —
And still in Stirling's royal park,
The gray-haired sires, who know the past,
To strangers point the Douglas-cast,[1]
And moralize on the decay
Of Scottish strength in modern day.

XXIV.

The vale with loud applauses rang,
The Ladies' Rock[2] sent back the clang.
The King with look unmoved, bestow'd
A purse well fill'd with pieces broad.
Indignant smiled the Douglas proud,
And threw the gold among the crowd,
Who now, with anxious wonder, scan,
And sharper glance, the dark gray man;
Till whispers rose among the throng,
That heart so free, and hand so strong,
Must to the Douglas blood belong;
The old men mark'd, and shook the head,
To see his hair with silver spread,
And wink'd aside, and told each son
Of feats upon the English done,
Ere Douglas of the stalwart hand
Was exiled from his native land.
The women praised his stately form,
Though wreck'd by many a winter's storm;

1 The throw made by Douglas.
2 A point from which the ladies of the court viewed the games.

The youth with awe and wonder saw
His strength surpassing nature's law.
Thus judged, as is their wont, the crowd,
Till murmur rose to clamors loud.
But not a glance from that proud ring
Of peers who circled round the King,
With Douglas held communion kind,
Or call'd the banish'd man to mind;
No, not from those who, at the chase,
Once held his side the honor'd place,
Begirt [1] his board, and, in the field,
Found safety underneath his shield;
For he, whom royal eyes disown,
When was his form to courtiers known!

XXV.

The Monarch saw the gambols flag,
And bade let loose a gallant stag,
Whose pride, the holiday to crown,
Two favorite greyhounds should pull down,
That venison free, and Bordeaux wine,
Might serve the archery to dine.
But Lufra, — whom from Douglas' side
Nor bribe nor threat could e'er divide,
The fleetest hound in all the North, —
Brave Lufra saw, and darted forth.
She left the royal hounds midway,
And dashing on the antler'd prey,
Sunk her sharp muzzle in his flank,
And deep the flowing lifeblood drank.
The King's stout huntsman saw the sport
By strange intruder broken short,
Came up, and with his leash unbound,
In anger struck the noble hound.

[1] Surrounded.

—The Douglas had endured, that morn,
The King's cold look, the nobles' scorn,
And last, and worst to spirit proud,
Had borne the pity of the crowd;
But Lufra had been fondly bred,
To share his board, to watch his bed,
And oft would Ellen, Lufra's neck
In maiden glee with garlands deck;
They were such playmates, that with name
Of Lufra, Ellen's image came.
His stifled wrath is brimming high,
In darken'd brow and flashing eye;
As waves before the bark divide,
The crowd gave way before his stride;
Needs but a buffet and no more,
The groom lies senseless in his gore.
Such blow no other hand could deal
Though gauntleted in glove of steel.

XXVI.

Then clamor'd loud the royal train,
And brandish'd swords and staves amain.
But stern the baron's warning—" Back !
Back, on[1] your lives, ye menial pack!
Beware the Douglas.—Yes! behold,
King James! The Douglas, doom'd of old,
And vainly sought for near and far,
A victim to atone the war,
A willing victim, now attends,
Nor craves thy grace but for his friends."—
" Thus is my clemency repaid ?
Presumptuous Lord !" the Monarch said;
" Of thy mis-proud[2] ambitious clan,

---

1 As you value.   2 Wrongly, mistakenly proud.

Thou, James of Bothwell, wert the man,
The only man, in whom a foe
My woman mercy would not know:
But shall a Monarch's presence brook
Injurious blow, and haughty look?—
What ho! the Captain of our Guard!
Give the offender fitting ward.—
Break off the sports!"— for tumult rose,
And yeomen 'gan to bend their bows,—
"Break off the sports!" he said, and frown'd,
"And bid our horsemen clear the ground."

XXVII.

Then uproar wild and misarray [1]
Marr'd the fair form of festal day.
The horsemen prick'd among the crowd,
Repell'd by threats and insult loud;
To earth are borne the old and weak,
The timorous fly, the women shriek;
With flint, with shaft, with staff, with bar,
The hardier urge tumultuous war.
At once round Douglas darkly sweep
The royal spears in circle deep,
And slowly scale the pathway steep;
While on the rear in thunder pour
The rabble with disorder'd roar.
With grief the noble Douglas saw
The Commons rise against the law,
And to the leading soldier said,—
"Sir John of Hyndford! [2] 'twas my blade
That knighthood on thy shoulder laid; [3]

---

[1] Disorder.   [2] A village on the Clyde.
[3] Knighthood was conferred by a slight blow with the flat of a sword on the back of the kneeling candidate.

For that good deed, permit me then
A word with these misguided men. —

XXVIII.

"Hear, gentle friends! ere yet for me
Ye break the bands of fealty.
My life, my honor, and my cause,
I tender free to Scotland's laws.
Are these so weak as must require
The aid of your misguided ire?
Or, if I suffer causeless wrong,
Is then my selfish rage so strong,
My sense of public weal so low,
That, for mean vengeance on a foe,
Those cords of love I should unbind,
Which knit my country and my kind?
Oh, no! Believe, in yonder tower
It will not soothe my captive hour,
To know those spears our foes should dread,
For me in kindred gore are red;
To know, in fruitless brawl begun
For me, that mother wails her son;
For me, that widow's mate expires;
For me, that orphans weep their sires;
That patriots mourn insulted laws,
And curse the Douglas for the cause.
Oh, let your patience ward [1] such ill,
And keep your right to love me still!"

XXIX.

The crowd's wild fury sunk again
In tears, as tempests melt in rain.
With lifted hands and eyes, they pray'd
For blessings on his generous head,

---

1 Ward off.

Who for his country felt alone,
And prized her blood beyond his own.
Old men, upon the verge of life,
Bless'd him who stayed the civil strife;
And mothers held their babes on high,
The self-devoted Chief to spy,
Triumphant over wrongs and ire,
To whom the prattlers owed a sire:
Even the rough soldier's heart was moved;
As if behind some bier beloved,
With trailing arms and drooping head,
The Douglas up the hill he led,
And at the Castle's battled verge,
With sighs resign'd his honor'd charge.

XXX

The offended Monarch rode apart,
With bitter thought and swelling heart,
And would not now vouchsafe again
Through Stirling streets to lead his train.—
"O Lennox, who would wish to rule
This changeling[1] crowd, this common fool?
Hear'st thou," he said, "the loud acclaim
With which they shout the Douglas name?
With like acclaim, the vulgar throat
Strain'd for King James their morning note;
With like acclaim they hail'd the day
When first I broke the Douglas' sway;
And like acclaim would Douglas greet,
If he could hurl me from my seat.
Who o'er the herd would wish to reign,
Fantastic, fickle, fierce, and vain!
Vain as the leaf upon the stream,
And fickle as a changeful dream;

[1] Fickle.

Fantastic as a woman's mood,
And fierce as Frenzy's fever'd blood,
Thou many-headed monster thing,
Oh, who would wish to be thy king!

XXXI.

"But soft! what messenger of speed
Spurs hitherward his panting steed?
I guess his cognizance [1] afar—
What from our cousin,[2] John of Mar?"—
"He prays, my liege, your sports keep bound
Within the safe and guarded ground:
For some foul purpose yet unknown,—
Most sure for evil to the throne,—
The outlaw'd Chieftain, Roderick Dhu,
Has summon'd his rebellious crew;
'Tis said, in James of Bothwell's aid
These loose banditti stand array'd.
The Earl of Mar, this morn, from Doune,
To break their muster march'd, and soon
Your grace will hear of battle fought;
But earnestly the Earl besought,
Till for such danger he provide,
With scanty train you will not ride."

XXXII.

"Thou warn'st me I have done amiss,—
I should have earlier look'd to this:
I lost it in this bustling day.
— Retrace with speed thy former way;
Spare not for spoiling of thy steed,
The best of mine shall be thy meed.

---

[1] Crest; livery.

[2] Monarchs frequently applied this epithet to their noblemen, even when
no blood relationship existed.

Say to our faithful Lord of Mar,
We do forbid the intended war:
Roderick, this morn, in single fight,
Was made our prisoner by a knight;
And Douglas hath himself and cause
Submitted to our kingdom's laws.
The tidings of their leaders lost
Will soon dissolve the mountain host,
Nor would we that the vulgar feel,
For their Chief's crimes, avenging steel.
Bear Mar our message, Braco: fly!"—
He turn'd his steed,—"My liege, I hie,—
Yet, ere I cross this lily lawn,
I fear the broadswords will be drawn."
The turf the flying courser spurn'd,
And to his towers the King return'd.

XXXIII.

Ill with King James's mood that day,
Suited gay feast and minstrel lay;
Soon were dismiss'd the courtly throng,
And soon cut short the festal song.
Nor less upon the sadden'd town
The evening sunk in sorrow down.
The burghers spoke of civil jar,
Of rumor'd feuds and mountain war,
Of Moray, Mar, and Roderick Dhu,
All up in arms:—the Douglas too,
They mourn'd him pent within the hold,
"Where stout Earl William [1] was of old."—
And there his word the speaker stayed,
And finger on his lip he laid,
Or pointed to his dagger blade.

[1] The Douglas who was stabbed by James II.

But jaded horsemen, from the west,
At evening to the Castle press'd;
And busy talkers said they bore
Tidings of fight on Katrine's shore;
At noon the deadly fray begun,
And lasted till the set of sun.
Thus giddy rumor shook the town,
Till closed the Night her pennons brown.

CANTO SIXTH.

THE GUARD ROOM.

I.

THE sun, awakening, through the smoky air
   Of the dark city casts a sullen glance,
Rousing each caitiff [1] to his task of care,
   Of sinful man the sad inheritance;
Summoning revelers from the lagging dance,
   Scaring the prowling robber to his den;
Gilding on battled tower the warder's lance,
   And warning student pale to leave his pen,
And yield his drowsy eyes to the kind nurse of men.

What various scenes, and, oh! what scenes of woe,
   Are witness'd by that red and struggling beam!
The fever'd patient, from his pallet low,
   Through crowded hospital beholds its stream;
The ruin'd maiden trembles at its gleam,
   The debtor wakes to thought of gyve and jail,
The lovelorn wretch starts from tormenting dream;
   The wakeful mother, by the glimmering pale,
Trims her sick infant's couch, and soothes his feeble wail.

1 Wretched, unfortunate man.

II.

At dawn the towers of Stirling rang
With soldier step and weapon clang,
While drums, with rolling note, foretell
Relief to weary sentinel.
Through narrow loop and casement barr'd,
The sunbeams sought the Court of Guard,
And, struggling with the smoky air,
Deaden'd the torches' yellow glare.
In comfortless alliance shone
The lights through arch of blacken'd stone,
And show'd wild shapes in garb of war,
Faces deform'd with beard and scar,
All haggard from the midnight watch,
And fever'd with the stern debauch;
For the oak table's massive board,
Flooded with wine, with fragments stored,
And beakers drain'd, and cups o'erthrown,
Show'd in what sport the night had flown.
Some, weary, snored on floor and bench;
Some labor'd still their thirst to quench;
Some, chill'd with watching, spread their hands
O'er the huge chimney's dying brands,
While round them, or beside them flung,
At every step their harness [1] rung.

III.

These drew not for their fields the sword,
Like tenants of a feudal lord,
Nor own'd the patriarchal claim
Of Chieftain in their leader's name;
Adventurers [2] they, from far who roved,

[1] Armor and other accouterments of war.

[2] James V. was the first to increase the army furnished by the nobles and their vassals by the addition of a small number of mercenaries.

To live by battle which they loved.
There the Italian's clouded face,
The swarthy Spaniard's there you trace;
The mountain-loving Switzer[1] there
More freely breathed in mountain air;
The Fleming[2] there despised the soil,
That paid so ill the laborer's toil;
Their rolls show'd French and German name;
And merry England's exiles came,
To share, with ill-conceal'd disdain,
Of Scotland's pay the scanty gain.
All brave in arms, well train'd to wield
The heavy halberd, brand, and shield;
In camps licentious, wild, and bold;
In pillage fierce and uncontroll'd;
And now, by holytide[3] and feast,
From rules of discipline released.

IV.

They held debate of bloody fray,
Fought 'twixt Loch Katrine and Achray.
Fierce was their speech, and, 'mid their words,
Their hands oft grappled to their swords;
Nor sunk their tone to spare the ear
Of wounded comrades groaning near,
Whose mangled limbs, and bodies gored,
Bore token of the mountain sword,
Though, neighboring to the Court of Guard,
Their prayers and feverish wails were heard;
Sad burden to the ruffian joke,
And savage oath by fury spoke! —
At length up started John of Brent,

[1] A native of Switzerland.
[2] An inhabitant of Flanders, as Belgium was then called.   [3] Holiday.

A yeoman from the banks of Trent;
A stranger to respect or fear,
In peace a chaser [1] of the deer,
In host [2] a hardy mutineer,
But still the boldest of the crew,
When deed of danger was to do.
He grieved, that day, their games cut short,
And marr'd the dicer's brawling sport,
And shouted loud, " Renew the bowl!
And, while a merry catch I troll,
Let each the buxom chorus bear,
Like brethren of the brand and spear."

v.

SOLDIER'S SONG.

Our vicar still preaches that Peter and Poule [3]
Laid a swinging [4] long curse on the bonny brown bowl,
That there's wrath and despair in the jolly black-jack, [5]
And the seven deadly sins in a flagon of sack; [6]
Yet whoop, Barnaby! off with thy liquor,
Drink upsees out, [7] and a fig for the vicar!

Our vicar he calls it damnation to sip
The ripe ruddy dew of a woman's dear lip,
Says, that Beelzebub [8] lurks in her kerchief so sly,
And Apollyon [8] shoots darts from her merry black eye;
Yet whoop, Jack! kiss Gillian the quicker,
Till she bloom like a rose, and a fig for the vicar!

Our vicar thus preaches — and why should he not?
For the dues of his cure are the placket and pot; [9]

---

[1] Poacher.   [2] War.   [3] Paul.   [4] Severe.
[5] A leathern beer jug.   [6] Spanish wine.
[7] " Upsees out," i.e., in the Dutch fashion, or deeply.
[8] Name for Satan.   [9] " Placket and pot," i.e., women and wine.

And 'tis right of his office poor laymen to lurch,
Who infringe the domains of our good Mother Church.
Yet whoop, bully-boys! off with your liquor,
Sweet Marjorie's the word, and a fig for the vicar!

VI.

The warder's challenge, heard without,
Stayed in mid-roar the merry shout.
A soldier to the portal went, —
" Here is old Bertram, sirs, of Ghent;
And, — beat for jubilee the drum! —
A maid and minstrel with him come."
Bertram, a Fleming, gray and scarr'd,
Was entering now the Court of Guard,
A harper with him, and in plaid
All muffled close, a mountain maid,
Who backward shrunk to 'scape the view
Of the loose scene and boisterous crew.
"What news?" they roar'd. — " I only know,
From noon till eve we fought with foe
As wild and as untamable
As the rude mountains where they dwell;
On both sides store of blood is lost,
Nor much success can either boast." —
" But whence thy captives, friend? such spoil
As theirs must needs reward thy toil.
Old dost thou wax, and wars grow sharp;
Thou now hast glee-maiden and harp!
Get thee an ape, and trudge the land,
The leader of a juggler band." —

VII.

" No, comrade; — no such fortune mine.
After the fight, these sought our line,
That aged Harper and the girl,

And, having audience of the Earl,
Mar bade I should purvey them steed,
And bring them hitherward with speed.
Forbear your mirth and rude alarm,
For none shall do them shame or harm."—
"Hear ye his boast?" cried John of Brent,
Ever to strife and jangling bent;
"Shall he strike doe beside our lodge,
And yet the jealous niggard grudge
To pay the forester his fee?
I'll have my share, howe'er it be,
Despite of Moray, Mar, or thee."
Bertram his forward step withstood;
And, burning in his vengeful mood,
Old Allan, though unfit for strife,
Laid hand upon his dagger knife;
But Ellen boldly stepp'd between,
And dropp'd at once the tartan screen:—
So, from his morning cloud, appears
The sun of May, through summer tears.
The savage soldiery, amazed,
As on descended angel gazed;
Even hardy Brent, abash'd and tamed,
Stood half admiring, half ashamed.

VIII.

Boldly she spoke,—"Soldiers, attend!
My father was the soldier's friend;
Cheer'd him in camps, in marches led,
And with him in the battle bled.
Not from the valiant, or the strong,
Should exile's daughter suffer wrong."—
Answer'd De Brent, most forward still
In every feat or good or ill,—
"I shame me of the part I play'd;

And thou an outlaw's child, poor maid!
An outlaw I by forest laws,
And merry Needwood [1] knows the cause.
Poor Rose, — if Rose be living now," —
He wiped his iron eye and brow, —
" Must bear such age, I think, as thou. —
Hear ye, my mates; — I go to call
The Captain of our watch to hall:
There lies my halberd on the floor;
And he that steps my halberd o'er,
To do the maid injurious part,
My shaft shall quiver in his heart! —
Beware loose speech, or jesting rough:
Ye all know John de Brent.   Enough."

IX.

Their Captain came, a gallant young, —
Of Tullibardine's [2] house he sprung, —
Nor wore he yet the spurs of knight;
Gay was his mien, his humor light,
And, though by courtesy controll'd,
Forward his speech, his bearing bold.
The high-born maiden ill could brook
The scanning of his curious look
And dauntless eye; — and yet, in sooth,
Young Lewis was a generous youth;
But Ellen's lovely face and mien,
Ill suited to the garb and scene,
Might lightly bear construction strange,
And give loose fancy scope to range.
" Welcome to Stirling towers, fair maid!
Come ye to seek a champion's aid,

1 A royal forest in Staffordshire.
2 Tullibardine was an old seat of the Murrays in Perthshire.

On palfrey white, with harper hoar,
Like errant damosel [1] of yore?
Does thy high quest [2] a knight require,
Or may the venture suit a squire?"—
Her dark eye flash'd;—she paused and sigh'd,—
"Oh, what have I to do with pride!—
Through scenes of sorrow, shame, and strife,
A suppliant for a father's life,
I crave an audience of the King.
Behold, to back my suit, a ring,
The royal pledge of grateful claims,
Given by the Monarch to Fitz-James."

X.

The signet ring young Lewis took,
With deep respect and alter'd look;
And said,—"This ring our duties own;
And pardon, if to worth unknown,
In semblance mean, obscurely veil'd,
Lady, in aught my folly fail'd.
Soon as the day flings wide his gates,
The King shall know what suitor waits.
Please you, meanwhile, in fitting bower
Repose you till his waking hour;
Female attendance shall obey
Your hest, for service or array.
Permit I marshal you the way."
But, ere she followed, with the grace
And open bounty of her race,
She bade her slender purse be shared
Among the soldiers of the guard.

---

[1] In the days of chivalry any oppressed "damosel" could obtain redress by applying to the court of the nearest king, where some knight became her champion.

[2] Undertaking.

The rest with thanks their guerdon took;
But Brent, with shy and awkward look,
On the reluctant maiden's hold
Forced bluntly back the proffer'd gold; —
" Forgive a haughty English heart,
And oh, forget its ruder part!
The vacant purse shall be my share,
Which in my barret cap I'll bear,
Perchance, in jeopardy of war,
Where gayer crests may keep afar."
With thanks — 'twas all she could — the maid
His rugged courtesy repaid.

XI.

When Ellen forth with Lewis went,
Allan made suit to John of Brent: —
" My lady safe, oh, let your grace
Give me to see my master's face!
His minstrel I, — to share his doom
Bound from the cradle to the tomb.
Tenth in descent, since first my sires
Waked for his noble house their lyres,
Nor one of all the race was known
But prized its weal above their own.
With the Chief's birth begins our care;
Our harp must soothe the infant heir,
Teach the youth tales of fight, and grace
His earliest feat of field or chase;
In peace, in war, our rank we keep,
We cheer his board, we soothe his sleep,
Nor leave him till we pour our verse —
A doleful tribute! — o'er his hearse.
Then let me share his captive lot;
It is my right — deny it not!" —
" Little we reck," said John of Brent,

" We Southern men, of long descent;
Nor wot we how a name — a word —
Makes clansmen vassals to a lord:
Yet kind my noble landlord's part, —
God bless the house of Beaudesert!
And, but I loved to drive the deer,
More than to guide the laboring steer,
I had not dwelt an outcast here.
Come, good old Minstrel, follow me;
Thy Lord and Chieftain shalt thou see."

XII.

Then, from a rusted iron hook,
A bunch of ponderous keys he took,
Lighted a torch, and Allan led
Through grated arch and passage dread.
Portals they pass'd, where, deep within,
Spoke prisoner's moan, and fetters' din;
Through rugged vaults, where, loosely stored,
Lay wheel, and ax, and headsman's sword,
And many an hideous engine grim,
For wrenching joint, and crushing limb,
By artist form'd, who deemed it shame
And sin to give their work a name.
They halted at a low-brow'd porch,
And Brent to Allan gave the torch,
While bolt and chain he backward roll'd,
And made the bar unhasp its hold.
They enter'd: — 'twas a prison room
Of stern security and gloom,
Yet not a dungeon; for the day
Through lofty gratings found its way,
And rude and antique garniture
Deck'd the sad walls and oaken floor;
Such as the rugged days of old

Deem'd fit for captive noble's hold.[1]
"Here," said De Brent, "thou mayst remain
Till the Leech[2] visit him again.
Strict is his charge, the warders tell,
To tend the noble prisoner well."
Retiring then, the bolt he drew,
And the lock's murmurs growl'd anew.
Roused at the sound, from lowly bed
A captive feebly raised his head;
The wondering Minstrel look'd, and knew —
Not his dear lord, but Roderick Dhu!
For, come from where Clan-Alpine fought,
They, erring, deem'd the Chief he sought.

XIII.

As the tall ship, whose lofty prore[3]
Shall never stem the billows more,
Deserted by her gallant band,
Amid the breakers lies astrand,[4]
So, on his couch, lay Roderick Dhu!
And oft his fever'd limbs he threw
In toss abrupt, as when her sides
Lie rocking in the advancing tides,
That shake her frame with ceaseless beat,
Yet cannot heave her from the seat; —
Oh, how unlike her course on sea!
Or his free step on hill and lea! —
Soon as the Minstrel he could scan,
"What of thy lady? — of my clan? —
My mother? — Douglas? — tell me all.
Have they been ruin'd in my fall?
Ah, yes! or wherefore art thou here?
Yet speak, — speak boldly, — do not fear."—

---

[1] Prison.   [2] Doctor.   [3] Prow.   [4] Stranded.

(For Allan, who his mood well knew,
Was choked with grief and terror too.)
"Who fought — who fled? — Old man, be brief; —
Some might — for they had lost their Chief.
Who basely live? — who bravely died?" —
"Oh, calm thee, Chief!" the Minstrel cried;
"Ellen is safe;" — "For that, thank Heaven!" —
"And hopes are for the Douglas given; —
The lady Margaret, too, is well;
And, for thy clan, — on field or fell,
Has never harp of minstrel told
Of combat fought so true and bold.
Thy stately Pine is yet unbent,
Though many a goodly bough is rent."

XIV.

The Chieftain rear'd his form on high,
And fever's fire was in his eye;
But ghastly, pale, and livid streaks
Checker'd his swarthy brow and cheeks.
— "Hark, Minstrel! I have heard thee play,
With measure bold, on festal day,
In yon lone isle, . . . again where ne'er
Shall harper play, or warrior hear! .
That stirring air that peals on high,
O'er Dermid's [1] race our victory. —
Strike it! — and then, (for well thou canst,)
Free from thy minstrel spirit glanced,
Fling me the picture of the fight,
When met my clan the Saxon might.
I'll listen, till my fancy hears
The clang of swords, the crash of spears!

[1] The Campbell clan. The Clan-Alpine, or the MacGregors, and the
Campbells, were hereditary enemies.

These grates, these walls, shall vanish then,
For the fair field of fighting men,
And my free spirit burst away,
As if it soar'd from battle fray."
The trembling Bard with awe obey'd,—
Slow on the harp his hand he laid;
But soon remembrance of the sight
He witness'd from the mountain's height,
With what old Bertram told at night,
Awaken'd the full power of song,
And bore him in career along;—
As shallop launch'd on river's tide,
That slow and fearful leaves the side,
But, when it feels the middle stream,
Drives downward swift as lightning's beam.

XV.

BATTLE OF BEAL' AN DUINE.

"The Minstrel came once more to view
The eastern ridge of Benvenue,
For ere he parted, he would say
Farewell to lovely Loch Achray—
Where shall he find, in foreign land,
So lone a lake, so sweet a strand!
   There is no breeze upon the fern,
     Nor ripple on the lake,
   Upon her eyry nods the erne,[1]
     The deer has sought the brake;
   The small birds will not sing aloud,
     The springing trout lies still,
   So darkly glooms yon thunder cloud,
   That swathes, as with a purple shroud,
     Benledi's distant hill.

[1] The sea eagle or osprey.

Is it the thunder's solemn sound
    That mutters deep and dread,
Or echoes from the groaning ground
    The warrior's measured tread ?
Is it the lightning's quivering glance
    That on the thicket streams,
Or do they flash on spear and lance
    The sun's retiring beams ?
I see the dagger crest of Mar,
I see the Moray's silver star,
Wave o'er the cloud of Saxon war,
That up the lake comes winding far !
    To hero bound for battle strife,
        Or bard of martial lay,
    'Twere worth ten years of peaceful life,
        One glance at their array!

XVI.

" Their light arm'd archers far and near
    Survey'd the tangled ground ;
Their center ranks, with pike and spear,
    A twilight forest frown'd ;
Their barbed [1] horsemen, in the rear,
    The stern battalia [2] crown'd.
No cymbal clash'd, no clarion rang,
    Still were the pipe and drum ;
Save heavy tread, and armor's clang,
    The sullen march was dumb.
There breathed no wind their crests to shake,
    Or wave their flags abroad ;
Scarce the frail aspen seem'd to quake,
    That shadow'd o'er their road.
Their vaward [3] scouts no tidings bring,
    Can rouse no lurking foe,

---

[1] Wearing defensive armor.   [2] Order of battle.   [3] Advance.

Nor spy a trace of living thing,
    Save when they stirr'd the roe;
The host moves like a deep-sea wave,
Where rise no rocks its pride to brave,
    High swelling, dark, and slow.
The lake is pass'd, and now they gain
A narrow and a broken plain,
Before the Trosachs' rugged jaws;
And here the horse and spearmen pause,
While, to explore the dangerous glen,
Dive through the pass the archer men.

XVII.

"At once there rose so wild a yell
Within that dark and narrow dell,
As all the fiends, from heaven that fell,
Had peal'd the banner cry of hell!
    Forth from the pass in tumult driven,
    Like chaff before the wind of heaven,
        The archery appear;
For life! for life! their plight they ply—
And shriek, and shout, and battle cry,
And plaids and bonnets waving high,
And broadswords flashing to the sky,
        Are maddening in the rear.
Onward they drive, in dreadful race,
    Pursuers and pursued;
Before that tide of flight and chase,
How shall it keep its rooted place,
    The spearmen's twilight wood?—
' Down, down,' cried Mar, ' your lances down!
    Bear back both friend and foe!'—
Like reeds before the tempest's frown,
That serried grove of lances brown
    At once lay level'd low;

And closely shouldering side to side,
The bristling ranks the onset bide. —
'We'll quell the savage mountaineer,
    As their Tinchel [1] cows the game!
They come as fleet as forest deer,
    We'll drive them back as tame.'—

XVIII.

"Bearing before them, in their course,
The relics of the archer force,
Like wave with crest of sparkling foam,
Right onward did Clan-Alpine come.
    Above the tide, each broadsword bright
    Was brandishing like beam of light,
        Each targe was dark below;
    And with the ocean's mighty swing,
    When heaving to the tempest's wing,
        They hurl'd them on the foe.
I heard the lance's shivering crash,
As when the whirlwind rends the ash;
I heard the broadsword's deadly clang,
As if an hundred anvils rang!
But Moray wheel'd his rearward rank
Of horsemen on Clan-Alpine's flank,
    —'My banner man, advance!
I see,' he cried, 'their column shake.—
Now, gallants! for your ladies' sake,
    Upon them with the lance!'—
The horsemen dash'd among the rout,
    As deer break through the broom;
Their steeds are stout, their swords are out,
    They soon make lightsome room.

[1] A circle of sportsmen surrounding a large space, which was gradually narrowed till the game it inclosed was brought within reach.

Clan-Alpine's best are backward borne —
 Where, where was Roderick then?
One blast upon his bugle horn
 Were worth a thousand men.
And refluent [1] through the pass of fear
 The battle's tide was pour'd;
Vanish'd the Saxon's struggling spear,
 Vanish'd the mountain sword.
As Bracklinn's chasm, so black and steep,
 Receives her roaring linn,
As the dark caverns of the deep
 Suck the dark whirlpool in,
So did the deep and darksome pass
Devour the battle's mingled mass:
None linger now upon the plain,
Save those who ne'er shall fight again.

XIX.

" Now westward rolls the battle's din,
That deep and doubling pass within.
— Minstrel, away! the work of fate
Is bearing on: its issue wait,
Where the rude Trosachs' dread defile
Opens on Katrine's lake and isle.
Gray Benvenue I soon repass'd,
Loch Katrine lay beneath me cast.
 The sun is set; — the clouds are met,
  The lowering scowl of heaven
 An inky hue of livid blue
  To the deep lake has given;
Strange gusts of wind from mountain glen
Swept o'er the lake, then sunk agen.
I heeded not the eddying surge,
Mine eye but saw the Trosachs' gorge,

---

[1] Flowing back.

Mine ear but heard that sullen sound,
Which like an earthquake shook the ground,
And spoke the stern and desperate strife
That parts not but with parting life,
Seeming, to minstrel ear, to toll
The dirge of many a passing soul.
    Nearer it comes — the dim-wood glen
The martial flood disgorged agen,
    But not in mingled tide;
The plaided warriors of the North
High on the mountain thunder forth
    And overhang its side;
While by the lake below appears
The dark'ning cloud of Saxon spears.
At weary bay each shatter'd band,
Eying their foemen, sternly stand;
Their banners stream like tatter'd sail,
That flings its fragments to the gale,
And broken arms and disarray
Mark'd the fell havoc of the day.

XX.

" Viewing the mountain's ridge askance,
The Saxon stood in sullen trance,
Till Moray pointed with his lance,
    And cried —' Behold yon isle! —
See! none are left to guard its strand,
But women weak, that wring the hand:
'Tis there of yore the robber band
    Their booty wont to pile; —
My purse, with bonnet pieces [1] store,
To him will swim a bowshot o'er,
And loose a shallop from the shore.

[1] A bonnet piece is an elegant gold coin, bearing on one side the head of
James V. wearing a bonnet.

Lightly we'll tame the war wolf then,
Lords of his mate, and brood, and den.' —
Forth from the ranks a spearman sprung,
On earth his casque and corselet rung,
      He plunged him in the wave: —
All saw the deed — the purpose knew,
And to their clamors Benvenue
      A mingled echo gave;
The Saxons shout, their mate to cheer,
The helpless females scream for fear,
And yells for rage the mountaineer.
'Twas then, as by the outcry riven,
Pour'd down at once the lowering heaven;
A whirlwind swept Loch Katrine's breast,
Her billows rear'd their snowy crest.
Well for the swimmer swell'd they high,
To mar the Highland marksman's eye;
For round him shower'd, 'mid rain and hail,
The vengeful arrows of the Gael. —
In vain — He nears the isle — and lo!
His hand is on a shallop's bow.
—Just then a flash of lightning came,
It tinged the waves and strand with flame; —
I mark'd Duncraggan's widow'd dame —
Behind an oak I saw her stand,
A naked dirk gleam'd in her hand:
It darken'd, — but, amid the moan
Of waves, I heard a dying groan;
Another flash! — the spearman floats
A weltering corse beside the boats,
And the stern matron o'er him stood,
Her hand and dagger streaming blood.

XXI.

"'Revenge! revenge!' the Saxons cried —
The Gael's exulting shout replied.
Despite the elemental rage,
Again they hurried to engage;
But, ere they closed in desperate fight,
Bloody with spurring came a knight,
Sprung from his horse, and, from a crag,
Waved 'twixt the hosts a milk-white flag.
Clarion and trumpet by his side
Rung forth a truce note high and wide,
While, in the Monarch's name, afar
An herald's voice forbade the war,
For Bothwell's lord, and Roderick bold,
Were both, he said, in captive hold."
— But here the lay made sudden stand,
The harp escaped the Minstrel's hand! —
Oft had he stolen a glance, to spy
How Roderick brook'd his minstrelsy:
At first, the Chieftain, to the chime,
With lifted hand, kept feeble time;
That motion ceased, — yet feeling strong
Varied his look as changed the song;
At length, no more his deafen'd ear
The minstrel melody can hear;
His face grows sharp, — his hands are clench'd,
As if some pang his heartstrings wrench'd;
Set are his teeth, his fading eye
Is sternly fix'd on vacancy;
Thus, motionless, and moanless, drew
His parting breath, stout Roderick Dhu! —
Old Allan-Bane look'd on aghast,
While grim and still his spirit pass'd:
But when he saw that life was fled,
He pour'd his wailing o'er the dead.

XXII.

LAMENT.

"And art thou cold and lowly laid,
Thy foeman's dread, thy people's aid,
Breadalbane's [1] boast, Clan-Alpine's shade!
For thee shall none a requiem say ? —
For thee, — who loved the Minstrel's lay,
For thee, of Bothwell's house the stay,
The shelter of her exiled line ?
E'en in this prison house of thine,
I'll wail for Alpine's honor'd Pine!

" What groans shall yonder valleys fill!
What shrieks of grief shall rend yon hill!
What tears of burning rage shall thrill,
When mourns thy tribe thy battles done,
Thy fall before the race was won,
Thy sword ungirt ere set of sun!
There breathes not clansman of thy line,
But would have given his life for thine.—
Oh, woe for Alpine's honor'd Pine!

"Sad was thy lot on mortal stage! —
The captive thrush may brook the cage,
The prison'd eagle dies for rage.
Brave spirit, do not scorn my strain!
And, when its notes awake again,
Even she, so long beloved in vain,
Shall with my harp her voice combine,
And mix her woe and tears with mine,
To wail Clan-Alpine's honor'd Pine."—

---

[1] The region bordering Loch Tay.

XXIII.

Ellen, the while, with bursting heart,
Remain'd in lordly bower apart,
Where play'd, with many-colored gleams,
Through storied [1] pane the rising beams.
In vain on gilded roof they fall,
And lighten'd up a tapestried wall,
And for her use a menial train
A rich collation spread in vain.
The banquet proud, the chamber gay,
Scarce drew one curious glance astray;
Or if she look'd, 'twas but to say,
With better omen dawn'd the day
In that lone isle, where waved on high
The dun deer's hide for canopy;
Where oft her noble father shared
The simple meal her care prepared,
While Lufra, crouching by her side,
Her station claim'd with jealous pride,
And Douglas, bent on woodland game,
Spoke of the chase to Malcolm Græme,
Whose answer, oft at random made,
The wandering of his thoughts betray'd.—
Those who such simple joys have known,
Are taught to prize them when they're gone.
But sudden, see, she lifts her head!
The window seeks with cautious tread.
What distant music has the power
To win her in this woeful hour!
'Twas from a turret that o'erhung
Her latticed bower, the strain was sung.

Stained or painted to form pictures illustrating history.

XXIV.

LAY OF THE IMPRISONED HUNTSMAN.

" My hawk is tired of perch and hood,
My idle greyhound loathes his food,
My horse is weary of his stall,
And I am sick of captive thrall.
I wish I were, as I have been,
Hunting the hart in forest green,
With bended bow and bloodhound free,
For that's the life is meet for me.

" I hate to learn the ebb of time,
From yon dull steeple's drowsy chime,
Or mark it as the sunbeams crawl,
Inch after inch, along the wall.
The lark was wont my matins ring,
The sable rook my vespers sing;
These towers, although a king's they be,
Have not a hall of joy for me.

" No more at dawning morn I rise,
And sun myself in Ellen's eyes,
Drive the fleet deer the forest through,
And homeward wend with evening dew;
A blithesome welcome blithely meet,
And lay my trophies at her feet,
While fled the eve on wing of glee, —
That life is lost to love and me!"

XXV.

The heart-sick lay was hardly said,
The list'ner had not turn'd her head,
It trickled still, the starting tear,
When light a footstep struck her ear.

And Snowdoun's graceful Knight was near.
She turn'd the hastier, lest again
The prisoner should renew his strain.
"Oh, welcome, brave Fitz-James!" she said;
"How may an almost orphan maid
Pay the deep debt"—"Oh, say not so!
To me no gratitude you owe.
Not mine, alas! the boon to give,
And bid thy noble father live;
I can but be thy guide, sweet maid,
With Scotland's King thy suit to aid.
No tyrant he, though ire and pride
May lay his better mood aside.
Come, Ellen, come! 'tis more than time—
He holds his court at morning prime."
With beating heart, and bosom wrung,
As to a brother's arm she clung.
Gently he dried the falling tear,
And gently whisper'd hope and cheer;
Her faltering steps half led, half stayed,[1]
Through gallery fair and high arcade,
Till, at his touch, its wings of pride
A portal arch unfolded wide.

XXVI.

Within 'twas brilliant all and light,
A thronging scene of figures bright;
It glow'd on Ellen's dazzled sight,
As when the setting sun has given
Ten thousand hues to summer even,
And from their tissue, fancy frames
Aërial[2] knights and fairy dames.
Still by Fitz-James her footing staid;

---

1 Supported.   2 Fanciful; imaginary.

A few faint steps she forward made,
Then slow her drooping head she raised,
And fearful round the presence [1] gazed;
For him she sought, who own'd this state,
The dreaded Prince, whose will was fate! —
She gazed on many a princely port,
Might well have ruled a royal court;
On many a splendid garb she gazed,
Then turn'd bewilder'd and amazed,
For all stood bare; and, in the room,
Fitz-James alone wore cap and plume.
To him each lady's look was lent;
On him each courtier's eye was bent;
Midst furs, and silks, and jewels sheen,
He stood, in simple Lincoln green,
The center of the glittering ring, —
And Snowdoun's Knight [2] is Scotland's **King.**

XXVII.

As wreath of snow, on mountain breast,
Slides from the rock that gave it rest,
Poor Ellen glided from her stay,
And at the Monarch's feet she lay;
No word her choking voice commands, —
She show'd the ring — she clasp'd her hands.
Oh! not a moment could he brook,
The generous Prince, that suppliant look!
Gently he raised her; and, the while,
Check'd with a glance the circle's smile;
Graceful, but grave, her brow he kiss'd,
And bade her terrors be dismiss'd: —

---

[1] Presence chamber of the King.

[2] James V. was accustomed to make personal investigation of the condition of his people. The name he generally assumed when in disguise was "Laird of Ballingeich."

"Yes, Fair; the wandering poor Fitz-James
The fealty of Scotland claims.
To him thy woes, thy wishes, bring;
He will redeem his signet ring.
Ask naught for Douglas; yestereven,
His Prince and he have much forgiven:
Wrong hath he had from slanderous tongue —
I, from his rebel kinsmen, wrong.
We would not, to the vulgar crowd,
Yield what they craved with clamor loud;
Calmly we heard and judged his cause,
Our council aided, and our laws.
I stanch'd thy father's death-feud stern
With stout De Vaux and gray Glencairn;
And Bothwell's Lord henceforth we own
The friend and bulwark of our Throne. —
But, lovely infidel, how now?
What clouds thy misbelieving brow?
Lord James of Douglas, lend thine aid;
Thou must confirm this doubting maid."

XXVIII.

Then forth the noble Douglas sprung,
And on his neck his daughter hung.
The Monarch drank, that happy hour,
The sweetest, holiest draught of Power, —
When it can say, with godlike voice,
Arise, sad Virtue, and rejoice!
Yet would not James the general eye
On Nature's raptures long should pry;
He stepp'd between — "Nay, Douglas, nay,
Steal not my proselyte away!
The riddle 'tis my right to read,
That brought this happy chance to speed.[1]

[1] Successful issue.

Yes, Ellen, when disguised I stray
In life's more low but happier way,
'Tis under name which veils my power;
Nor falsely veils — for Stirling's tower
Of yore the name of Snowdoun claims,
And Normans call me James Fitz-James.
Thus watch I o'er insulted laws,
Thus learn to right the injured cause." —
Then, in a tone apart and low, —
" Ah, little traitress! none must know
What idle dream, what lighter thought,
What vanity full dearly bought,
Join'd to thine eye's dark witchcraft, drew
My spellbound steps to Benvenue,
In dangerous hour, and all but gave
Thy Monarch's life to mountain glaive!" —
Aloud he spoke, — "Thou still dost hold
That little talisman of gold,
Pledge of my faith, Fitz-James's ring —
What seeks fair Ellen of the King?"

XXIX.

Full well the conscious maiden guess'd
He probed the weakness of her breast;
But, with that consciousness, there came
A lightening of her fears for Græme,
And more she deem'd the Monarch's ire
Kindled 'gainst him, who, for her sire,
Rebellious broadsword boldly drew;
And, to her generous feeling true,
She craved the grace of Roderick Dhu.
" Forbear thy suit: — the King of kings
Alone can stay life's parting wings.
I know his heart, I know his hand,
Have shared his cheer, and proved his brand; —

My fairest earldom would I give
To bid Clan-Alpine's Chieftain live!—
Hast thou no other boon to crave?
No other captive friend to save?"
Blushing, she turn'd her from the King,
And to the Douglas gave the ring,
As if she wish'd her sire to speak
The suit that stain'd her glowing cheek.—
"Nay, then, my pledge has lost its force,
And stubborn Justice holds her course.—
Malcolm, come forth!"—and, at the word,
Down kneel'd the Græme to Scotland's Lord.
"For thee, rash youth, no suppliant sues,
From thee may Vengeance claim her dues,
Who, nurtured underneath our smile,
Hast paid our care by treacherous wile,
And sought, amid thy faithful clan,
A refuge for an outlaw'd man,
Dishonoring thus thy loyal name.—
Fetters and warder for the Græme!"—
His chain of gold the King unstrung,
The links o'er Malcolm's neck he flung,
Then gently drew the glittering band,
And laid the clasp on Ellen's hand.

Harp of the North, farewell! The hills grow dark,
   On purple peaks a deeper shade descending;
In twilight copse the glowworm lights her spark,
   The deer, half seen, are to the covert wending.
Resume thy wizard elm! the fountain lending,
   And the wild breeze, thy wilder minstrelsy;
Thy numbers sweet with Nature's vespers blending,
   With distant echo from the fold and lea,
And herd-boy's evening pipe, and hum of housing [1] bee.

1 Returning to the hive.

Yet, once again, farewell, thou Minstrel Harp!
  Yet, once again, forgive my feeble sway!
And littie reck I of the censure sharp
  May idly cavil at an idle lay.
Much have I owed thy strains on life's long way,
  Through secret woes the world has never known,
When on the weary night dawn'd wearier day,
  And bitterer was the grief devour'd alone.
That I o'erlived such woes, Enchantress! is thine own.

Hark! as my lingering footsteps slow retire,
  Some Spirit of the Air has waked thy string!
'Tis now a seraph bold, with touch of fire —
  'Tis now the brush of Fairy's frolic wing.
Receding now, the dying numbers ring
  Fainter and fainter down the rugged dell,
And now the mountain breezes scarcely bring
  A wandering witch note of the distant spell —
And now, 'tis silent all! — Enchantress, fare thee well!

GLOSSARY.

ARCADE. A series of arches supported by columns or piers, either open or backed by masonry.

AUGURY. 1. The art or practice of foretelling events. 2. An omen or prediction.

BARRET CAP. A kind of cap or head gear formerly worn by soldiers.

BATTLEMENT. A wall or rampart around the top of a castle, with openings to look through and annoy the enemy.

BLACK-JACK. A capacious drinking cup or can formerly made of waxed leather.

BRACKEN. Large coarse fern.

BULWARK. A rampart; a fortification.

CARPET KNIGHT. A person knighted on some other ground than that of military service; a knight who has not known the hardships of war.

CLOSE. To grapple; to come to close quarters in fight.

COIF. A kind of cap worn by Scottish matrons.

CREST. 1. The plume or decoration on the top of a helmet. 2. The device over a coat of arms. 3. The ridge of the neck of a horse or dog.

DICER. A gamester.

DRAWBRIDGE. A bridge at the entrance of a castle, which, when lowered by chains, gave access across the moat or ditch surrounding the structure.

EMBOSSED. (A technical hunting term.) Flecked or spotted with foam.

FAVOR. Something which was bestowed as a token of good will or of love, as a glove or a knot of ribbon, to be worn habitually by a knight-errant.

FEINT. (A technical fencing term.) A seeming aim at one part when it is intended to strike another.

FEUDAL. Pertaining to that political form in which there was a chain of persons holding land of one another on condition of performing certain services. Every man in the chain was bound to his immediate superior, held land from him, took oath of allegiance to him, and became his man.

FLOURISH. A trumpet call; a fanfare or prelude by one or more trumpets performed on the approach of any person of distinction.

FRONTLET. The front of a stag's head; the horns.

GUARD. In fencing, a position of passive defense.

HALBERD. A long-handled weapon armed with a steel point, and having a crosspiece of steel with a cutting edge.

HENCHMAN. A groom; an attendant or follower.

JACK. An upper garment of leather, worn for defense by common soldiers. It was sometimes strengthened by small pieces of metal stitched into it.

JENNET. A small Spanish horse.

KEN. Sight; knowledge.

LAW. "To give law" to a stag is to allow it a start of a certain distance or time before the hounds are slipped, the object being to insure a long chase.

MEW. A cage for hawks while mewing or moulting: hence an inclosure, a place of confinement.

PASS. (A term in fencing.) To thrust with a sword.

PENNON. A swallow-tailed flag or streamer.

POLEAX. An ax fixed to a pole or handle. It was formerly used by mounted soldiers.

PRIME. In the Roman Catholic Church the first canonical hour of prayer, six o'clock in the morning, generally the first quarter of the day.

QUARTERSTAFF. A stout staff used as a weapon of defense. In using it, one hand was placed in the middle, and the other halfway between the middle and the end.

SIGNET. 1. A seal. 2. A ring containing a signet or private seal.

SLIP. To let slip; to loose hands from the noose; to be sent in pursuit of game.

SQUIRE. An attendant upon a knight.

STIRRUP CUP. A cup of wine drunk on parting from a friend on horseback.

STORE. (An obsolete adjective.) Accumulated; stored up.

STRATH. A valley of considerable size, through which a river flows.

TARGE. Target-shield.

TINEMAN. An officer of the forest, who had the nocturnal care of vert and venison.

TROLL. 1. A song the parts of which are sung in succession; a round. 2. To sing in the manner of a catch or round, also in a full, jovial voice.

VAIR. The skin of the squirrel, much used in the fourteenth century as fur for garments.

VANTAGE COIGN. A position of advantage for observing or operating.

WARD. A guarding or defensive position or motion in fencing.

WARDER. One who wards or keeps

WHINYARD. A short sword or knife

SUGGESTIONS FOR STUDY.

The Lady of the Lake is usually read in the first year of the high school course, and it is with this fact in mind that the following suggestions have been made. It is an excellent book with which to begin the study of the ordinary forms of poetry, of plot structure, and the simpler problems of description. For this reason in the exercises that follow the emphasis has been placed on these topics.

THE POEM.

The Lady of the Lake is an excellent example of the minor epic. Corresponding to the "Arms and the man I sing," of the Æneid, and the invocation to the Muse, are the statement of the theme, "Knighthood's dauntless deed and Beauty's matchless eye," and the invocation to the Harp of the North, in the opening stanzas. For the heroes, descendants of the gods, of the great epic, we have a king, the chieftain of a great clan, an outlaw earl and his daughter, characters less elevated than those of the great epic, but still important. The element of the supernatural brought in by the gods and goddesses of the epic is here supplied by the minstrel, Brian the priest, and the harp. The interest of the poem lies in the incidents as with the epic. The romantic story of Ellen and Malcolm, however, lies quite outside the realm of the great epic, which is concerned with the fate of a state or body of people rather than with that of an individual.

THE PLOT.

There are two threads to the story, one concerned with the love story of Ellen and Malcolm, the main plot; and one with Roderick and his clan against the King, the minor plot. The connection between them is very slight, the story of Ellen could have been told almost without the other, but the struggle of the Clan makes a fine background for the love story of Ellen and Malcolm. The plot is an excellent one for the beginner to study as the structure is so evident. The following is a simple outline of the main incidents of the story.

I. The complication:
   1. The coming of the stranger, later supposed by Roderick to be a spy of the King.
   2. The return of Douglas, guided by Malcolm, an act which brings Malcolm under the displeasure of the King.
   3. Roderick's proposal for Ellen's hand in order to avert the danger threatening Ellen and Douglas because of the recognition of the latter by the King's men.
   4. The rejection of the proposal, leading to the withdrawal of Ellen and her father to Coir-Uriskin and the departure of Douglas to the court to save Roderick and Malcolm.
   5. The preparations for war made by Roderick, including the sending of the Fiery Cross, and the Taghairm.

II. The height or climax.
   1. Ellen and Allan-Bane at Coir-Uriskin.
   2. Douglas on his way to give himself up.
   3. Malcolm in prison for aiding Douglas.

III. The turning point in the plot.
   1. The coming of Fitz-James.
   2. The giving of the ring.
   3. The gay music of the harp.

IV. The unraveling of the plot.
   1. The triumph of Fitz-James over Roderick.
   2. The interest reawakened in the King by Douglas's prowess and generosity.
   3. The arrival of Ellen at the court.
   4. The battle of Beal 'an Duine.
   5. Roderick's death.
   6. The freeing of Malcolm.
   7. The restoration of the Douglases.

SCOTT'S USE OF DESCRIPTION.

All of Scott's works afford excellent models of description for the beginner in this very difficult form of composition. He deals with the problems of description in a simple and evident manner. In most cases he begins his description with the point of view, and chooses the details in accordance with that point of view. The principle of order used in the arrangement of the details is usually easy to find and follow, and the beauty of his contrasts, the vanity and vividness of his diction can be in a measure appreciated even by boys and girls in the first year of the high school. If properly taught a pupil must leave the study of the poem with a new sense of the power of words. In his description of character Scott deals with the most simple and elemental emotions and is therefore fairly easy to imitate. In the special topics under each canto special emphasis has been laid upon description because of the adaptability of *his* description to the needs of the student.

SPECIAL STUDIES IN THE CANTOS.

CANTO I.

I. Poetic forms.
  1. The Spenserian Stanza.
  2. Meter of the poem.
  3. Meter and stanza of "Soldier, rest."
II. Description. Stanzas XI to XVI.
  1. Use of significant words: strong, harsh words to describe a wild and rugged scene, *thunder-splintered*, *huge*, etc.; vivid and color words to describe glowing beauty, *gleaming*, *living gold*, etc.
  2. Use of onomatopœia.
  3. Order in arrangement of details. Stanza XI, etc.
  4. Use of contrast. Stanzas XI, XII, XV, etc.
  5. Variety of expression. Note synonymous expressions for *grew*, Stanza XII.
  6. Unity with point of view. Stanza XXVI.
III. Plot structure.
  1. Events of first canto.
IV. Character study.
  1. Ellen: Fitz-James.
    a. Characteristics given by Scott.
    b. Characteristics displayed in action.

Other Topics.

V. Means of suggesting the mystery which usually accompanies romance.
   1. The scene.
      a. "So wondrous wild. . . .
         The scenery of a fairy dream."
      b. "Nor think you unexpected come," etc.
      c. The falling sword.
      d. The dream.

VI. Means used to excite interest.
   1. Concealment of Ellen's and Lady Margaret's identity.
   2. The dream.
   3. The Douglas?

CANTO II.

I. Verse forms.
   1. Meter of the songs in the canto.

II. Plot structure.
   1. Method of telling what is necessary for reader to know of preceding events, or exposition.
      a. Story of the Douglases.
      b. Story of Roderick Dhu.
   2. Introduction of minor plot.
   3. Events in main plot.
   4. Connection between the two plots.

III. Character study.
   1. Characteristics of Ellen not seen in Canto I.
   2. Allan-Bane.
   3. Malcolm, the typical young knight of romance.
      a. Justification of Scott's characterization of Malcolm by his actions in this canto.
   4. Douglas.
   5. Roderick Dhu.

CANTO III.

I. Verse forms.
   1. Meter and stanza of songs in the canto.

II. Description.
    1. Of morning.
        a. Impression given by description.
    2. Of the Goblin-cave.
        a. Means used to give effect of gruesomeness.

III. Plot structure.
    1. Events of main plot.
    2. Events of minor plot.
    3. Connection between the two plots.

Other Topics.

IV. Means used to make the ceremonial of the Fiery Cross "fraught with deep and deathful meaning."
    1. Materials used.
        a. For the fire.
        b. For the cross.
    2. Brian.
        a. Appearance.
        b. Parentage.
        c. Mode of life.
        d. Supernatural powers.
    3. The curses.
    4. Responses to the curses.
        a. On part of people.
        b. On part of nature.

V. Means used to give the impression of swiftness in Malise's race.

CANTO IV.

I. Verse forms.
    1. The Ballad.
        a. Stanza and meter.
        b. Subject.

II. Plot structure.
    1. The climax; the height of Ellen's misfortunes.
    2. Hints of a fortunate outcome for Ellen.
    3. Introduction of means for unraveling the plot.
        a. The gift of the ring.

      4. Hints of an unfortunate outcome for Roderick.

      5. Use of the Taghairm in the story.

      6. Part played by Blanche of Devon.

III. Character study.

      1. Roderick as "father of the clan."

      2. Justification of characterization of Fitz-James in Canto I by events of Canto IV.

Other Topics.

  V. The hospitality of the Highlanders.

CANTO V.

I. Plot structure.

      1. Events of main plot.

      2. Events of minor plot.

      3. Connection between the two.

II. Character study.

      1. Roderick.

      2. The King.

      3. Douglas.

      4. The mob.

        a. The King's characterization.

Other Topics.

III. Justice of Roderick's justification of himself to Fitz-James.

IV. Means used to give the impression of speed in Fitz-James's ride.

  V. Exemplification in this canto of the line, "Shine martial Faith, and Courtesy's bright star!"

CANTO VI.

I. Description.

      1. Morning.

        a. Contrast between this and that in Canto III.

        b. Reason for difference.

      2. The guard room.

        a. Point of view.

        b. Choice of details.

    3. The dungeon of romance.

    4. The battle.

        a. Use of contrast.

        b. Use of onomatopœia.

        c. Picturesque incidents.

        d. Advantage of description by an onlooker.

II. Plot structure.

    1. The surprise.

        a. Previous hints as to the identity of James.

    2. The happy ending.

        a. Justification.

III. Character study.

    1. Ellen in the guard room.

    2. The King.

TOPICS FOR COMPOSITION.

    1. Customs of the Highlanders.

    2. Two Ideas of Hospitality.

    3. The Knight of Romance.

    4. The Lady of Romance.

    5. The Heroine of To-day.

    6. The Modern Knight.

    7. Methods of Highland Warfare.

    8. Roderick Dhu as a General.

    9. The Scottish Minstrel.

    10. Was James a Good King?

    11. Dramatization of a Scene from *The Lady of the Lake.*

    12. The Kind of Man Scott Admired.

    13. Dreams That Came True.

    14. Superstitions.

ECLECTIC ENGLISH CLASSICS

Addison's Sir Roger de Coverley Papers (Underwood)

Arnold's Sohrab and Rustum (Tanner)

Bunyan's Pilgrim's Progress (Jones and Arnold)

Burke's Conciliation with America (Clark)
  Speeches at Bristol (Bergin)

Burns's Poems—Selections (Venable)

Byron's Childe Harold (Canto IV), Prisoner of Chillon, Mazeppa, and other Selections (Venable)

Carlyle's Essay on Burns (Miller)

Chaucer's Prologue and Knighte's Tale (Van Dyke)

Coleridge's Rime of the Ancient Mariner (Garrigues)

Cooper's Pilot (Watrous)
  The Spy (Barnes)

Defoe's History of the Plague in London (Syle)
  Robinson Crusoe (Stephens)

De Quincey's Revolt of the Tartars

Dickens's Christmas Carol and Cricket on the Hearth (Wannamaker)
  Tale of Two Cities (Pearce)

Dryden's Palamon and Arcite (Bates)

Eliot's Silas Marner (McKitrick)

Emerson's American Scholar, Self-Reliance, Compensation (Smith)

Franklin's Autobiography (Reid)

Goldsmith's Vicar of Wakefield (Hansen)
  Deserted Village (See Gray's Elegy)

Gray's Elegy in a Country Churchyard, and Goldsmith's Deserted Village (Van Dyke)

Hughes's Tom Brown's School Days (Gosling).

Irving's Sketch Book—Selections (St. John)
  Tales of a Traveler (Rutland)

Lincoln's Addresses and Letters (Moores)
  Address at Cooper Union (See Macaulay's Speeches on Copyright)

Macaulay's Essay on Addison (Matthews)
  Essay on Milton (Mead)

Macaulay's Essays on Lord Clive and Warren Hastings (Holmes)
Lays of Ancient Rome and other Poems (Atkinson)
Life of Johnson (Lucas)
Speeches on Copyright, and **Lincoln's** Address at Cooper Union (Pittenger)

Milton's L'Allegro, Il Penseroso, Comus, Lycidas (Buck)
Paradise Lost. Books I and II (Stephens)

Old Ballads (Morton).

Old Testament Narratives (Baldwin)

Poe's Selected Poems and Tales (Stott)

Pope's Homer's Iliad. Books I, VI, XXII, and XXIV
Rape of the Lock and Essay on Man (Van Dyke)

Ruskin's Sesame and Lilies (Rounds)

Scott's Abbot
Ivanhoe (Schreiber)
Lady of the Lake (Bacon)
Marmion (Coblentz)
Quentin Durward (Norris)
Woodstock

Shakespeare's As You Like It (North)
Hamlet (Shower)
Henry V (Law)
Julius Cæsar (Baker)
Macbeth (Livengood)
Merchant of Venice (Blakely)
Midsummer Night's Dream (Haney)
The Tempest (Barley).
Twelfth Night (Weld)

Southey's Life of Nelson

Stevenson's Inland Voyage and Travels with a Donkey (Armstrong)
Treasure Island (Fairley)

Swift's Gulliver's Travels (Gaston)

Tennyson's Idylls of the King—Selections (Willard)
Princess (Shryock)

Thackeray's Henry Esmond (Bissell)

Washington's Farewell Address, and **Webster's** First Bunker Hill Oration (Lewis)

Webster's Bunker Hill Orations (See also **Washington's** Farewell Address)

Wordsworth's Poems—Selections (Venable)

ADVERTISEMENTS

HALLECK'S NEW ENGLISH LITERATURE

By REUBEN POST HALLECK, M. A., LL. D.
author of History of English Literature, and History of American Literature.

THIS New English Literature preserves the qualities which have caused the author's former History of English Literature to be so widely used; namely, suggestiveness, clearness, organic unity, interest, and power to awaken thought and to stimulate the student to further reading.

¶ Here are presented the new facts which have recently been brought to light, and the new points of view which have been adopted. More attention is paid to recent writers. The present critical point of view concerning authors, which has been brought about by the new social spirit, is reflected. Many new and important facts concerning the Elizabethan theater and the drama of Shakespeare's time are incorporated.

¶ Other special features are the unusually detailed Suggested Readings that follow each chapter, suggestions and references for a literary trip to England, historical introductions to the chapters, careful treatment of the modern drama, and a new and up-to-date bibliography.

¶ Over 200 pictures selected for their pedagogical value and their unusual character appear in their appropriate places in connection with the text. The frontispiece, in colors, shows the performance of an Elizabethan play in the Fortune Theater.

AMERICAN BOOK COMPANY

S. 90)

A HISTORY OF AMERICAN LITERATURE

By REUBEN POST HALLECK, M.A.,
Principal, Male High School, Louisville, Ky.

A COMPANION volume to the author's History of English Literature. It describes the greatest achievements in American literature from colonial times to the present, placing emphasis not only upon men, but also upon literary movements, the causes of which are thoroughly investigated. Further, the relation of each period of American literature to the corresponding epoch of English literature has been carefully brought out—and each period is illuminated by a brief survey of its history. ¶ The seven chapters of the book treat in succession of Colonial Literature, The Emergence of a Nation (1754-1809), the New York Group, The New England Group, Southern Literature, Western Literature, and the Eastern Realists. To these are added a supplementary list of less important authors and their chief works, as well as A Glance Backward, which emphasizes in brief compass the most important truths taught by American literature. ¶ At the end of each chapter is a summary which helps to fix the period in mind by briefly reviewing the most significant achievements. This is followed by extensive historical and literary references for further study, by a very helpful list of suggested readings, and by questions and suggestions, designed to stimulate the student's interest and enthusiasm, and to lead him to study and investigate further for himself the remarkable literary record of American aspiration and accomplishment.

AMERICAN BOOK COMPANY
(S.318)

TEACHERS', OUTLINES FOR STUDIES IN ENGLISH

Based on the Requirements for Admission to College

By GILBERT SYKES BLAKELY, A.M., Instructor in English in the Morris High School, New York City.

THIS little book is intended to present to teachers plans for the study of the English texts required for admission to college. These Outlines are full of inspiration and suggestion, and will be welcomed by every live teacher who hitherto, in order to avoid ruts, has been obliged to compare notes with other teachers, visit classes, and note methods. The volume aims not at a discussion of the principles of teaching, but at an application of certain principles to the teaching of some of the books most generally read in schools.

¶ The references by page and line to the book under discussion are to the texts of the Gateway Series; but the Outlines can be used with any series of English classics.

¶ Certain brief plans of study are developed for the general teaching of the novel, narrative poetry, lyric poetry, the drama, and the essay. The suggestions are those of a practical teacher, and follow a definite scheme in each work to be studied. There are discussions of methods, topics for compositions, and questions for review. The lists of questions are by no means exhaustive, but those that are given are suggestive and typical.

¶ The appendix contains twenty examinations in English, for admission to college, recently set by different colleges in both the East and the West.

AMERICAN BOOK COMPANY

(S.87)

WEBSTER'S SECONDARY SCHOOL DICTIONARY

Full buckram, 8vo, 864 pages. Containing over 70,000 words, with 1000 illustrations.

THIS NEW DICTIONARY is based on Webster's New International Dictionary and therefore conforms to the best present usage. It presents the largest number of words and phrases ever included in a school dictionary —all those, however new, likely to be needed by any pupil. It is a reference book for the reader and a guide in the use of English, both oral and written. It fills every requirement that can be expected of a dictionary of moderate size.

¶ This new book gives the preference to forms of spelling now current in the United States. In the matter of pronunciation such alternatives are included as are in very common use. Each definition is in the form of a specific statement accompanied by one or more synonyms, between which careful discrimination is made.

¶ In addition, this dictionary includes an unusual amount of supplementary information of value to students: the etymology, syllabication and capitalization of words; many proper names from folklore, mythology, and the Bible; a list of prefixes and suffixes; all irregularly inflected forms; rules for spelling; 2329 lists of synonyms, in which 3518 words are carefully discriminated; answers to many questions on the use of correct English constantly asked by pupils; a guide to pronunciation; abbreviations used in writing and printing; a list of 1200 foreign words and phrases; a dictionary of 5400 proper names of persons and places, etc.

AMERICAN BOOK COMPANY
(S. 105)